# Nine lectures on Leonardo da Vinci

edited by
Francis Ames-Lewis
with the assistance of
Anka Bednarek

Department of History of Art
Birkbeck College
University of London

## Photographic acknowledgements

1000091226

| | |
|---|---|
| Hamburg, Kunsthalle | 17 |
| London, Christie's | 4, 5 |
| Madrid, Biblioteca Nacional | ill.B |
| Milan, Sorintendenza per i Beni artistici e storici | front cover; 6, 7, 8, 9, 10, 11 |
| Oxford, The Governing Body of Christ Church | 1 |
| Turin, Biblioteca Reale | 18 |
| Windsor Castle, Royal Library © Her Majesty the Queen | back cover; 2, 3, 12, 13, 14, 15, 16, ill.A, ill.C |

# Contents

## Editorial Note

In conjunction with this book, the reader should for the most part use the plates in the catalogue of the *Leonardo da Vinci: Artist - Scientist - Inventor* exhibition held at the Hayward Gallery, London, in Spring 1989 (hereafter 'Catalogue 1989'). Plates in this catalogue are here referred to in bold characters, thus: **(32)** indicates a catalogue entry number, and **(fig.23)** a supporting illustration.

References are also often made to illustrations and texts in other catalogues, in anthologies of Leonardo da Vinci's writings, and in standard monographs on Leonardo. These works are cited in 'short form' (author and year of publication only) in the text; full references are listed in the select bibliography on p.109-10.

# Introduction

"Leonardo emphasised again and again in his writings that the art of painting had to rest on knowledge. To him the widespread ignorance of the fundamental truth, that there was no art without science, was responsible for the low esteem in which his chosen profession was too often held. Far from being a mere craft, painting should be classified with the so-called Liberal Arts, the disciplines based on knowledge... Without a profound understanding of the laws of nature the artist could never become the very rival of the Creator as Leonardo wished him to be." (Catalogue 1989, pp.1-2)

Thus wrote Sir Ernst Gombrich in his introduction to the catalogue of the Leonardo da Vinci exhibition held at the Hayward Gallery, London, in spring 1989. Reflecting Leonardo's views on the intimate relationship between art and science, the exhibition concentrated on exemplifying through his drawings and writings Leonardo's keen sense of the inner unity of all of creation. A greater number of Leonardo's drawings than had ever been assembled for an exhibition before illustrated the immense range of Leonardo's activities as an artist who was profoundly concerned with the workings of Nature in all its manifestations. And conversely, they also showed how Leonardo drew both to stimulate and to record his explorations of the forms and the phenomena of the natural world.

The exhibition thus demonstrated the whole range of functions of Leonardo's drawings. At the 'pure science' end of this spectrum, drawings showed his activity as a conscientious recorder of the fine details of an anatomical dissection, or as an experimental physicist writing up his experiment with the aid of brilliantly perceptive and skilful diagrams. Other drawings, often detailed records of direct observations of natural forms, showed Leonardo at work as a geologist, or as scrutineer of the world of animals and plants. Yet another group demonstrated his versatile abilities in applying these empirical observations: in mechanical engineering formulating new or improved systems of gearing or new machine tools, in hydraulics developing pumps and water-raising screws, in military engineering inventing novel types of artillery and armoured vehicles, or in cartography establishing new conventions and increased accuracy in mapping and in topographical record-making.

Leonardo's work as an artist can sometimes appear to have been submerged beneath his extensive and fertile range of activities in what we now characterise as the pure and applied sciences. But another aspect of his genius that the exhibition demonstrated with considerable success is that his artistic activities were critically informed by his work in scientific investigation, just

7

as the latter depended on his skills as a draughtsman. In his studies of human anatomy and physiology, for instance, he could scarcely have made (let alone recorded) such subtle discriminations between the manifold parts of the body had it not been for his long training in visual and perceptual skills which were in the Renaissance a vital part of a painter's apprenticeship. It is in this sense that all facets of Leonardo's activities are complementary, and that his 'science' and his 'art' are symbiotic and fully interdependent.

This interdependence, which lies at the heart of Leonardo's intellectual processes, was admirably shown by the arrangement of the exhibition into sections each of which was devoted to an aspect of Leonardo's general intellectual preoccupations. If any one facet of Leonardo's endeavours was less thoroughly illuminated, however, both because of problems of access to appropriate loans and because of the intellectual thrust that the exhibition organisers wished to bring to bear on the material exhibited, it was that for which (rightly or wrongly) he is perhaps best known: his career as an artist. Thus it was that the Department of History of Art at Birkbeck College, University of London, mounted a series of lectures entitled 'Aspects of Leonardo the Artist'.

As it turned out, these were the only public lectures offered in London during the spring of 1989 specifically in connection with the Hayward Gallery exhibition. The hope was that this series would encourage listeners to amplify and to feed off experiences gained by visiting the exhibition; and would, furthermore, complement the exhibition by concentrating less on the range of Leonardo's explorations of phenomena of the natural world than on his application of these preoccupations in his artistic creativity and achievements. Many of those who followed the lecture course in its entirety, and joined in the discussion after each lecture, appear to have believed that these goals were to a large degree realised. Many commented favourably on the range and consistently thought-provoking quality of the lectures; and many also suggested that to make them available to a wider audience would be a valuable contribution to the generalist literature on Leonardo da Vinci.

This volume is the result of the interest voiced by these individuals. Just as the lectures themselves were conceived with a lay audience in mind, so these studies of aspects of Leonardo's artistic activity are offered essentially to students and interested laypeople, rather than to scholars or specialists in the art of Leonardo and his contemporaries. One or two of these lectures will be published in more detailed form in academic journals or elsewhere; and ideas generated in others derive from, or may be reworked in other contexts into, more detailed scholarly research than is to be found here. As they stand in this volume, however, the lectures are intended to be accessible to a broad spectrum of readers, whose only qualification needs to be an interest in the extraordinary flexibility of Leonardo da Vinci's mind and in the brilliant dexterity of the his hand.

To the seven lectures of the Birkbeck College series, two others have been

8

added. In collaboration with the National Gallery, London, the Birkbeck College Centre for Extra-Mural Studies set up in March 1989 a Study Day at which a group of art historians and conservators presented papers on Leonardo's art and on the problems of restoration that his works may pose; one of these papers is reprinted here. Finally, thanks to the generous agreement of the President of the Leonardo da Vinci Society, of the lecturer himself, and of the Director of the Italian Cultural Institute, it has been possible to include the 1989 Annual Lecture delivered to the Leonardo da Vinci Society and to a large and catholic audience drawn together at the Italian Institute in London on 21 March 1989. In this lecture, Dr Pietro Marani, of the Pinacoteca di Brera in Milan, reported on the results of the current programme of restoration of the *Last Supper* in the Refectory of Sta Maria delle Grazie, and the implications of this restoration for our understanding of Leonardo the artist.

A word of explanation is necessary about the illustration of these lectures. I decided at the outset that since many of Leonardo da Vinci's works are so well-known and so frequently illustrated it was not necessary to incorporate herein a large number of reproductions of familiar images. On the other hand, it was clear that illustrations of the results of restoration work on the *Last Supper*, reproduced in colour, were essential. A number of black-and-white reproductions of less familiar, and less easily accessible, works have also been included. For the most part, however, this book must be used in conjunction with the 1989 Hayward Gallery exhibition catalogue, which has an unrivalled collection of excellent colour plates of Leonardo's paintings and drawings.

Finally, I have several acknowledgements to make. First, to the 'prime movers' of the 1989 Leonardo da Vinci exhibition, Professor Martin Kemp (University of St Andrews) and Jane Roberts (Royal Library, Windsor Castle), without whose imagination and energetic perseverance in overcoming the hurdles of mounting an exhibition of the complexity of this one there would have been no specific reason for the majority of these lectures to have been delivered. I am indebted to them, too, for contributing to the lecture series and to this volume. Second, to all the other contributors as well, for their help in preparing their texts and in discussing issues of bibliography and illustration with me. Third, to my colleagues in the Birkbeck College Department of History of Art both for their encouragement and for their agreement to underwrite this in-house publishing venture, the first of its type that we have undertaken. And finally, to my assistants Sally Smith (for help at the initial stages) and especially Anka Bednarek, who has taken up the challenges inherent in production and publication of this book with enthusiasm and energy.

Francis Ames-Lewis

# Leonardo da Vinci: motions of life in the lesser and greater worlds

"Motion is the cause of all life" (MS.H³, 141r)

Leonardo was one of those people who are virtually unable to look at one thing in isolation without realising its actual and potential associations with a complex nexus of other things. All the multifarious structures and phenomena in the visible world - whether falling under the purviews of anatomy or astronomy, geology or geometry, botany or ballistics, or whatever discipline - seemed to him to participate in a special kind of living unity, a unity which resided in the universal operation of the laws of cause and effect. This dynamic unity was perceived both intuitively and intellectually.

Although it would be oversimplifying his intellectual development to say that he began by sensing the affinities between forms in motion on the basis of artistic intuitions and ended by analyzing the underlying basis of motion in scientific terms, it is clear that he placed ever-increasing emphasis upon the need for a minutely rigorous analysis of form and function in all the myriad creations of nature. This point can be illustrated by comparing drawings of the same kinds of subjects from near the beginning and end of his career.

Already in his famous drawing of the Val d'Arno (**fig.14**) produced in 1473 when he was twenty-one years old, he has been able to express a remarkable sense of nature as 'process'. What could have been a flatly descriptive record of Tuscan topography has been transformed into a living evocation of motion, whether it is the material motion of tangible substances, as in the cascade of water from the right-hand cliff, or the sensory motion of the eye as it explores the plunging distances. A few scrawled perspective lines in the background suggest the passage of space towards worlds beyond our vision. If we set this drawing beside one of the studies of the river Adda in Lombardy (**20**), drawn in 1513 while he was staying at the family villa of his favourite pupil, Francesco Melzi, the same perception of the life of the earth is clearly apparent. However, a close scrutiny of the later drawing, which is executed with a miniaturist's delicacy of touch, indicates a more precisely structured approach to the way in which the elements behave in relation to each other, both in natural situations and in man's contrivances as an engineer. This more structured approach is founded upon years of study of water in motion, of erosion and of man's efforts to tame the powers of nature.

A comparable but less obvious parallel can be drawn when we look at his treatment of drapery, taking as our points of comparison the earliest of his surviving studies (**plate 1**) for a detail in a known painting, the sleeve of the angel in the Uffizi *Annunciation*, and the extraordinarily complex drawing in pen, black wash, black chalk and white heightening on red-prepared paper (56) for the sleeve of the Virgin in the *Virgin, Child, St Anne and a Lamb* in the Louvre. The drawings are again separated in date by as much as forty years. The earlier drawing is already characterised by a lively sense of rhythm in the fluttering ribbon and in the implicit spirals formed by the bunched cloth around the arm, but these configurations do not differ significantly in kind from the mobile draperies favoured by a number of artists in the Florentine tradition, including his master, Andrea del Verrocchio. The later drawing not only employs much more complex, layered effects of translucent material but also exploits his sense of the ubiquitous nature of vortex motion in a far more self-conscious manner. The draperies are not actually in spiral motion as such, but they are the product of competing forces of compression and expansion which cause the static folds to settle into configurations similar to those of dynamic currents in turbulent water or air. Leonardo's own famous parallel between the motion of water and the curling of hair (to be quoted later) makes it clear that there were deep structural affinities within the worlds of statics and dynamics.

My primary intention in this lecture is to look at the way in which Leonardo articulated his intuitive sense of the life of the world into conscious, analytical form. I will use as my key his characterisation of five different kinds of 'immaterial' motion in nature, but, before I do so, I think we should remind ourselves of the rationale underlying his search for universal principles in natural and human design. The rationale lay in the time-honoured analogy between the microcosm and macrocosm - or the lesser and greater worlds. His formulations of this notion have been much quoted in the literature, but in order to ensure that we set his views in their proper context, we will be justified in repeating a typical passage:

"Man has been called by the ancients a lesser world, and certainly the award of this name is well deserved, because, as much as man is composed of earth, water, air and fire, the body of the earth is similar; if man has in himself the bones, the supports and armature for the flesh, the world has the rocks, the supports of the earth; if man has within himself the lake of the blood, in which the lungs increase and decrease in breathing, the body of the earth has its oceanic sea, which likewise increases and decreases every six hours with the breathing of the world; if from the said lake veins arise, which proceed to ramify throughout the human body, the oceanic sea fills the body of the earth with infinite veins of water; the nerves are lacking in the body of the earth - they are not there because nerves are made for the purpose of movement, and the world, being perpetually immobile, does not need movement... But in all other respects they are very similar." (MS.A, 55v)

11

At the literal heart of this analogy is the role of mobile fluids in the life of the lesser (human) world and in the overall life of the greater world of the macrocosm. Leonardo's personal development of the analogy is above all concerned with the dynamics of motion - not simply the obvious aspects of physical motion but also the varieties of motion found in every phenomenon which occurs in time and space, whether material or immaterial. In addition to the obvious material motion of physical objects, he defined five kinds of immaterial motions:

> "The first is called temporal because it is concerned solely with the movement of time and embraces within itself all the others; the second is the life of things; the third is called mental and resides in animated bodies; the fourth is the images of things, which diffuse through the air as light rays (this class does not appear to be subject to time...); the fifth is that of sounds which go through the air, also odours and tastes and those things called sensory motions." (CA, 203va)

All of these are apparent directly or indirectly in the Adda study (**20**). Time is metaphorically represented by the transit of the ferry across its cable, which serves as a linear measure of its progress across the impetuous currents of water. The dynamic interplay of rocks and water may be taken as representative of 'the life of things'. The outward effects of 'mental motions' are apparent in the actions of the man on the ferry, who appears to be labouring an ox with a stick. The sense of elusive impressions of half-seen details is just one of the phenomena which result from the diffusion of light through the air. And 'sensory motions' are present by implication at least in the sounds of the turbulent water and of the stranded ox at the lower right, apparently crying after its companions.

The five varieties of motion were all governed by the same series of interlocking laws. These laws were discernible by the artist-scientist in terms of the arithmetical and geometrical ratios which governed the performance and design of all things: "proportion is not only to be found in number and measure, but also in sounds, weights, times and places and in every potency which exists" (MS.K, 49r). In exploring this concept, and seeing how he is able to express it in visual terms, I intend to reverse Leonardo's order of the five motions, working from the more specific to the general.

### 1. Sensory motions of the non-visual kind

Given the huge priority Leonardo placed upon sight - characterising it as a sense apart in his descriptions of the varieties of motion - the remaining senses of hearing, touch, taste and smell were of secondary concern to him. But this did not mean that he could dismiss them as falling outside the rule of universal law. Even fragrance, he conjectured, was governed by harmonics "similar to music" (Madrid II, 67r), though we may sense his frustration that the transmission of odours across space was not readily susceptible to the kind of mathematical analysis he applied to vision. Two of the senses, taste and touch, were obviously not available to spatial analysis since they "come into contact with their objects" and "can only gain knowledge from this direct contact" (Urb, 4v). By contrast, sound can be shown to behave with a mathematical regularity akin to that of light, radiating from its source in a manner which resembles concentric ripples in water and diminishing in strength at greater distances from its source according to a fixed series of ratios (expressed by Leonardo as a pyramidal law). However, in practice, the ear could not perceive this 'perspective of sound' as reliably as the eye can perceive distance through visual perspective:

> "The ear is strongly subject to delusions about the location and distance of its objects because the images [of sounds] do not reach it in straight lines, like those of the eye, but by tortuous and reflexive lines. Many times things that are remote sound closer than those nearby, on account of the way in which the images are transmitted." (Urb, 4v; Kemp/Walker 1989, p.18)

Even if the temporal motion of sound across space did not fully match the mathematical regularity of light, our instantaneous perception of harmonies of sound could nonetheless be regarded as closely equivalent to our appreciation of the visual beauties of proportion:

> "Music... composes harmony from the conjunction of her proportional parts, which make their effect instantaneously, being constrained to arise and die in one or more harmonic intervals. These intervals may be said to circumscribe the proportionality of the component parts of which such harmony is composed - no differently from the linear contours of the limbs from which human beauty is generated." (Urb, 16r-v; Kemp/Walker 1989, p.34)

## 2. The motion of light

The behaviour of light in space and the supreme receptivity of the eye were central to Leonardo's theory and practice of art, and indeed provided the bases on which he proclaimed the superiority of painting over all other arts and of visual experience over purely mental speculation in all human endeavours. The harmonic ratios enjoyed by the eye consisted not only in shapes and figures, analogous to those of musical chords, but also in regular spatial progressions which could be registered by the eye in an instant (in contrast to the temporal progress of a musical composition which could only be comprehended sequentially):

> "Although the objects in front of the eye touch each other as if hand in hand, I shall none the less found my rule on a scale of 20 for 20 *braccia*, just as the musician has done with notes. Although the notes are united and attached to each other, he has none the less recognised small intervals between note and note, designating them as first, second, third, fourth and fifth, and in this manner from interval to interval has given names to the varieties of raised and lowered notes." (BN 2038, 23r; Kemp/Walker 1989, pp.34-5)

The visual 'scale' which provides the basis for this analogy is that of geometrical perspective, which shows how objects of equal size undergo apparent diminution according to fixed ratios when located further away from the spectator at successive intervals:

> "I have found by experiment that when the second object is as far from the first as the first is from the eye, although they are the same size, the second will appear as half as small as the first. And if the third object is as far distant from the second as the second is from the eye, it will appear half the size of the second, and so on by degrees." (BN 2038, 23r; Urb, 146v-7r; Kemp/Walker 1989, p.57)

The analogy between the proportional diminution of images across space and the behaviour of sound is developed in more physical terms when he considers the patterns of diffusion: "every body placed in an illuminated atmosphere diffuses itself circularly and fills the surrounding area with infinite images of itself", just as "sound moves to disperse itself circularly" and as "a stone flung into water becomes the centre and cause of various circles." (MS.A, 9v)

Such analogies between the behaviour of optical and material phenomena could take unexpected turns in Leonardo's thought. Having recorded unexceptionably that shadows are darker nearer the objects casting them, he goes on to note that:

> "Shadow shares the nature of universal things, which are all more powerful at their beginning and become enfeebled towards their end. When I speak about the beginning of every form and quantity, discernible and indiscernible, I do not refer to things arising from small beginnings that become greatly enlarged over a period of time, as will happen with a great oak which has a

modest start in a little acorn. Rather I mean that the oak is strongest at the point at which it arises from the earth, that is to say where it has its greatest thickness. Correspondingly darkness is the first degree of shadow and light is the last. Therefore, painter, make your shadow darker close to its origin, and at its end show it being transformed into light, that is to say, so that it appears to have no termination." (BN 2038, 21v; Urb, 175r-v)

When he turned his attention to the perceptual apparatus with which man has been provided for the reception of such visual effects, Leonardo accorded the eye both a privileged design and a privileged relationship with the brain. The eye itself was envisaged, as it had been in medieval theory, as a complex optical instrument constructed from spheres and part-spheres of transparent humours of various refractive properties. Although his conception of the precise arrangement of the humours and of the paths of light rays within the eye was subject to continual revision, the basic principle of the geometrical perfection of the eye as an optical device remained unshaken. This instrument stood in a special relationship to the brain's ventricles, within which he believed the mental processes to occur. In some of his hypothetical schemes for the arrangement of the ventricles with their respective mental faculties he showed the optic nerves communicating with the intellect by a different route from the 'lower' senses. In his most famous diagram of the ventricles (**94**), the eye appears virtually as a bud or extrusion from the brain, in keeping with his characterisation of the eye as 'the window of the soul'.

## 3. Mental motions

In addition to their receptive and analytical capacities, the ventricles of the brain also contained the faculty which was responsible for voluntary motion, the physical manifestation of the third of Leonardo's categories. When, in the period around 1490, he began to explore the perceptual system of the brain, he also began to investigate the system by which commands were transmitted from the brain to the peripheral regions. The system he adopted was traditional, in that the nerves were conceived as 'perforated chords' which "carry commands and sensations to all the operative limbs; these chords command movement among the muscles and sinews." (Windsor 19019r; Clark/Pedretti 1969, p.10). Below one of his diagrams of the deep-lying network of neural 'chords' in the neck and shoulder, he stressed the relevance of such studies to the artist: "this demonstration is as necessary to good draughtsmen as is the origin of words from Latin for good grammarians." (Windsor 19021v; Clark/Pedretti 1969, p.11). Throughout the whole of the human body the 'chords' ramify like branches and roots to form a 'tree' (his precise term). The commands of the brain are transmitted through this ramifying system in such way that every aspect of a figure's motion and

15

expression responds to the 'motions of the mind'. It is this vision of the mind and body as a dynamic and expressive continuum that finds expression in the agitated reactions of the disciples in the *Last Supper* and in the terrified grimaces of the combatants in his *Battle of Anghiari* (**fig.32**):

> "Make the conquered and beaten pale, with their brows knit high and let the skin above be heavily furrowed with pain. Let the sides of the nose be wrinkled in an arch starting at the nostrils... which cause these crease lines, and the lips arched to reveal the upper teeth... parted as if to wail in lamentation." (BN 2038, 31r-30v; Urb, 53r-v; Kemp/Walker 1989, p.229)

As always with Leonardo, the description of emotion is made compelling and at the same time distanced by the analytical tone with which he assesses the causes and effects. It is altogether characteristic of his desire to achieve an orderly understanding of 'mental motions' that he should have attempted to place them within a system of classification:

> "Motions are of three kinds, that is to say motion of place and motion by simple action, and the third is motion composed of motion by action and motion of place... Motion of place is when the animal moves from one location to another. Motion by action is the motion that the animal makes in the same place without change of location. Motion of place is of three kinds, that is to say, rising, falling and going on the level. These three are supplemented by two, namely slowness and speed, and by two others, that is to say, straight motion and twisting motion, and another related one, that is to say, jumping." (Urb, 111r-v; Kemp/Walker 1989, pp.132-3)

We can sense his difficulties as he starts with a simple set of three categories, and then progressively realises that he has to introduce further variables if his system is to embrace the complexities of bodies in motion. The difficulties for the observer are further compounded by the realisation that even a single, simple 'motion by action' can be envisaged at any of the theoretically infinite intervals between its commencement and its completion (**97**; detail, **plate 2**):

> "The movements of man during the course of a single event are infinitely varied in themselves. The proof is as follows. In the case of a man delivering a blow to some object... the motion occurs across space and... the space will be a continuous quantity and every continuous quantity is infinitely divisible. Hence it is concluded that every motion of something which descends is infinitely variable." (Urb, 110v; Kemp/Walker 1989, p.133)

16

## 4. The motion of the life of things

Although the motions of the body commanded by mental urgings may give the 'semblance' of life to other things - as when the aviator operates the levers, pedals and pulleys of his flying machine - these 'mental motions' are actually the symptoms of life rather than its cause. The 'life of things', Leonardo's second category, results from the mysterious and inexorable action of the invisible and immaterial forces of the world, as the elements and material bodies move in a constant turmoil of chain reactions and percussive impacts:

> "Force is an immaterial power [*virtù spirituale*], an invisible potency which is infused by accidental violence in all bodies located outside their natural balance... giving to these bodies the semblance of life. This life is of marvellous efficiency, compelling and transmuting all created things from their places and shapes... It lives by violence and dies through liberty... Great power gives it great desire for death. It drives away with fury whatever opposes its self-destruction... Nothing moves without it. No sound or voice is heard without it." (CA, 302vb)

Leonardo devoted immense energies to the understanding of the behaviour of this 'immaterial power' in the lesser and greater worlds, searching for the dynamic laws which would explain the visual patterns of the elements in motion. Of the four elements, water most occupied his attention. It was more mobile than earth; its motions were more visible than those of air; and it had a weight and tangibility absent from evanescent fire. Water provided the perfect manifestation of the inexorable nature of force in the natural world:

> "Moving water strives to maintain the course pursuant to the power which occasions it, and if it finds an obstacle in its path, it completes the span of the course it has commenced by circular and revolving movement." (MS.A, 60r)

The language and tone of this passage is typical of Leonardo's characterisation of the elements when set in motion. He talks of their 'desire' and 'will' to complete their assigned motion and to find their assigned level in the order of things. Although he is obviously not thinking in terms of mental intentions, it is clear that he is endowing the elements with a kind of purposive 'life' - or, as we shall see, a 'quintessence'.

The property which determines that all mobile elements complete the due span of the 'life' with which they have been endowed was called 'impetus'. Leonardo derived this term from the theories of medieval dynamics to be found in the writings of such philosophers as Oresme, Bradwardine and

Buridan. The amount of impetus infused in an object determined how far it must travel before the force was expended. When he described the dynamic vortices of water in his drawings (61) Leonardo was in effect drawing lines of force in accordance with the degrees of impetus of the individual currents of water, as they compete violently with each other and with the imprisoned bubbles of air, which 'desire' to burst to the surface and end their lives 'in liberty'.

Such motions could be overwhelmingly destructive, as in the cataclysms of his 'Deluge' drawings (22, 63-4, 66, and Windsor 12379, 12381-86; Clark/Pedretti 1968, pp.54-5); or, when contained and harnessed, they could generate the life-giving properties of heat, growth and action. This life-giving potential is apparent at the heart of the microcosm:

> "This earth has a spirit of growth, and the flesh is the soul; its bones are the successive strata of rocks which form the mountains; its cartilage is the tufa stone; its blood the springs of the waters. The lake of blood which lies within the heart is its ocean. Its breathing is by the increase of the blood in its pulses and even so in the earth is the ebb and flow of the sea."
> (Hammer, 34r)

It is surely this shared spirit of life in the body of the earth and the human body that explains at least part of the enduring potency of the *Mona Lisa* (fig.4). The painting is suffused throughout with outer echoes of inner life, whether we look at the facial expression of the lady or at the tortuous rivulets of water and hair:

> "Observe the motion of the surface of water, which resembles the behaviour of hair, which has two motions, of which one depends on the weight of the strands, the other on the line of its revolving; thus water makes revolving eddies, one part of which in part depends upon the impetus of the principal current, and the other depends on the incident and reflected motions." (Windsor 12579r; Catalogue 1989, p.124)

The configurations of spirals and vortices which he recognised so ubiquitously in these and many other effects in nature - including the arrangement of branches around the stems of plants - resulted from the combining of a simple motion or weight acting in a straight line with a sequence of progressive deflections caused by forces or resistances acting across or against the main impetus. The vortex was a form of dynamic geometry across space and time.

Leonardo devoted enormous efforts to the investigation of the analogous structures with which the lesser and greater worlds have been endowed in

18

order to act in concert with such fundamental patterns of motion. One typical question that occupied his attention over a wide period of time was the reason for the way in which 'veins of water' trapped within the earth sometimes burst out as mountain springs, high above the natural level for water. Not surprisingly he sought explanations by referring to the way in which the pressure of the blood ensures that it reaches the head of a standing man. Although in the very last phases of his thought he came to realise the limits and even the fallacies in this method of argument, the idea of design by analogy played a central role in his theory and practice for much of his career. Thus, when he came to consider how a new city should be designed, he conceived its structures and its circulatory systems - particularly the networks of canals and sewers - much as if he were designing the body of a natural organism.

Alternatively, when he sought to understand natural structures, he analyzed their design as if they were the products of mathematical engineering. The valves of the heart (**plate 3**), for example, were characterised as perfect pieces of mechanical design, which use the laws governing the transformation of geometrical shapes to exploit the geometrical vortices of blood in the necks of the vessels. The ultimate proof would be the building of a model by the human engineer to achieve exactly the same effects, and this is precisely what Leonardo planned to do in this instance, as is shown by the notes and diagrams on the illustrated sheet. In this vision of the design of the natural world, the principles of geometry in motion and the organic structures of anatomical forms operate in complete harmony with each other.

## 5. The motion of time

The motions we see in the body of the earth in the background of the *Mona Lisa* differ from those of machines in one major respect. Although a machine may be subject to wear and may eventually break down, the principle of a machine's operation is that its action should be repeatable many times without significant variation. By contrast, the motions of the fluids which 'vivify' the body of the earth act inexorably to transform the structure of the earth. Over the long term, awesome transformations have occurred. The study of the topography of the Arno valley which Leonardo undertook during his work on schemes of canalization led him to appreciate that vast changes had shaped the landscape:

"In the great valley of the Arno above Gonfolina, a rock which was in ancient times united with Monte Albano in the form of a great bank... kept the river pent up in such a way that before it could flow into the sea, which was then at the foot of this rock, it formed two great lakes, of which the first is where today we see the city of Florence flourishing together with Prato and

Pistoia... From the Val d'Arno up as far as Arezzo a second lake was created, into which the aforesaid lake discharged its waters. It was closed near where Girone is seen today and occupied all of that upper valley for a distance of 40 miles in length... This lake was joined with the lake of Perugia." (Hammer, 9r)

Through great geological transformations, the motion of time - the first and most fundamental of Leonardo's varieties of motion - may be said to assume physical form. As a lesser world, the human frame was no more exempt from its effects than the body of the world:

"O time, consumer of all things, O envious age. You destroy all things and consume all things with the hard teeth of old age, little by little in slow death. Helen, looking at her reflection, observing the withered wrinkles made in her face by old age, wept and contemplated why it was that she had twice been abducted." (CA, 71ra)

The ineluctable destiny of man was shared with the elements themselves:

"Now see that the hope and desire of returning to the first chaos seem like the moth to the light, and that the man who, with constant desire, always awaits with joy the new spring, always the new summer, always the months - the things he desires seemingly coming too late - does not realise that he is willing his own destruction; but this desire is the very quintessence of the elements, which, finding itself trapped within the soul of the human body, always desires to return to its giver. And you should know that this same desire is that quintessence, and the man is a model of this world." (BL, 156v)

The irresistible nature of this desire or 'quintessence' for a return to the 'first chaos' is nowhere more vividly expressed than in the 'Deluge' drawings (e.g. 66), in which his scientific visions of impetus and vortex motion are placed in the service of awesome images of destruction. Such motions owe their origins to the 'Prime Mover', the ineffable and immaterial agency which was ultimately responsible for disrupting the elements by removing them from their natural places of rest. The 'Prime Mover' may be seen as the metaphorical hand which has stirred the mobile elements in the universal bucket into an apparently endless motion. But the motion was only apparently endless. The implication of Leonardo's vision may be that the impetus of the 'Prime Mover' would itself be expended in due course and that the elements would finally settle into stable, concentric configurations around the centre of the earth. In the meantime:

"We do not lack ways or devices of dividing and measuring these
miserable days of ours, wherein it should be our pleasure that
they be not frittered away or passed over in vain, without leaving
behind any memory of ourselves in the mind of man."
(CA, 12va)

Although we may sense Leonardo's own frustrations at the march of time,
which left so many cherished projects unfulfilled, he has triumphantly
succeeded - through the brilliance of the vision expressed in his surviving
manuscripts, drawings and handful of paintings - in leaving an indelible
'memory... in the mind of man'. We need make no apology for continuing to
celebrate that memory in this set of published lectures.[1]

Martin Kemp

1. Abbreviated references to Leonardo's manuscripts are given in the standard form, as
in Kemp/Walker 1989, pp.317-8; see also p.109, below.

# Leonardo and tradition

A better title for this lecture might be 'Leonardo's visual sources', for that is mostly what I am going to talk about, but I wanted to stress that many of the problems that Leonardo confronted, and many of the enterprises he embarked upon, find their places in a whole sequence of efforts for which the word 'tradition' is a useful abbreviation.[1] And it is well to remember that Leonardo himself was an art historian, even if, from his surviving writings, a laconic one. In the *Paragone*, for example, he refers to Luca della Robbia and the invention of glazed terracotta, and he discusses also the qualities of *schiacciato* relief, not naming Donatello but revealing the knowledge of his work that can be demonstrated from his paintings. These passing observations were not merely that - they found a place within what was clearly a developed historical scheme in Leonardo's mind. The following quotation comes from the Codex Atlanticus:

> "the painter will produce pictures of little excellence if he takes other painters as his authority, but if he learns from natural things he will bear good fruit. We saw this in the painters who came after the Romans. They always imitated each other and their art went ever into decline from one age to the next. After these came Giotto the Florentine who was not content to copy the works of his master Cimabue... He began to copy upon the stones the movements of the goats whose keeper he was... in such a way that after much study he surpassed not only all the masters of his age but all those of many centuries before. After this, art fell back into decline, because everyone copied the pictures that had already been done, and thus from century to century the decline continued until Tomaso the Florentine, nicknamed Masaccio, showed to perfection in his work how those who take as their authority any other than nature, mistress of the masters, labour in vain." (CA, 387r; Kemp-Walker 1989, p.193)

In embryo here we have the three-part division of Vasari's *Lives*, with Giotto and Masaccio seen as the first two great steps prior to Leonardo himself: a conclusion Leonardo modestly did not mention.

Leonardo's awareness of the past should encourage us to think of him in context, but this is not easy. The protean display of his genius, the legends

---

[1] I have made a few alterations and additions to the text of my lecture given on 23 February 1989, but its substance remains identical. There seems little point in burdening the text with footnotes, but I have added one or two references and asides that seem to me of interest.

that surround him, and that began in his lifetime, make him an extraordinarily difficult artist to approach. As Vasari wrote:

> "In the normal course of events many men and women are born with various remarkable qualities and talents; but occasionally, in a way that transcends nature, a single person is marvellously endowed by heaven with beauty, grace, and talent in such abundance that he leaves other men far behind, all his actions seem inspired, and indeed everything he does clearly comes from God rather than from human art.
>
> Everyone acknowledged that this was true of Leonardo da Vinci, an artist of outstanding physical beauty who displayed infinite grace in everything he did and who cultivated his genius so brilliantly that all problems he studied he solved with ease. He possessed great strength and dexterity; he was a man of regal spirit and tremendous breadth of mind; and his name became so famous that not only was he esteemed during his lifetime but his reputation endured and became even greater after his death."
> (Vasari/Bull 1965, p.255)

This is intimidating: how can we approach such a superhuman being? I think that this problem characterises a great deal of what has been written on Leonardo: general syntheses, minute studies of aspects of his work and thought, share - obviously with exceptions - a tendency to isolate Leonardo from his time and training, from his artistic contemporaries and predecessors - sometimes to their devaluation.[2] To take one example from a book I greatly admire, the late Lord Clark's classic monograph: Verrocchio - the most inventive quattrocento Florentine sculptor after Donatello, one of the greatest of draughtsmen, a designer of extraordinary inventiveness - is seen as an important influence on Leonardo, but he is dealt with in about a page and a half (Clark 1976, pp.20-2). His stature is thereby much reduced and his pervading effect on his pupil's work long after his death is hardly taken into account. Thus, as far as I am aware, it has not been pointed out - it certainly is not noted in the Windsor catalogue - that in one of Leonardo's most famous drawings, the design for a masque costume of around 1513 (**78**) the figure is posed as a repetition of Verrocchio's bronze *David* (Pope-Hennessy

---

[2] Leonardo's sources have received increasing attention recently, notably in C. Gould *Leonardo, the Artist and the non-Artist*, London 1975, and Kemp, 1981. For Leonardo and the antique see K. Clark, "Leonardo and the Antique" in C.D. O'Malley ed., *Leonardo's Legacy*, Berkeley, California, 1969, pp.1-34, and M. Kemp and A. Smart, "Leonardo's Leda and the Belvedere *River-Gods*: Roman Sources and a new Chronology", *Art History* III, 1980, pp.182-193; for his interest in Northern art, P. Hills, "Leonardo and Flemish Art", *Burlington Magazine* CXXII, 1980, pp.609-15.

1971, pl.79), executed exactly half a century earlier.[3] The art-historical passage by Leonardo quoted above seems to have been written about 1500, when Leonardo returned to Florence after his long stay in Milan. In 1501 he exhibited a famous cartoon - now lost but known through copies of which the most accurate is probably the painting by Brescianino formerly in the Gemäldgalerie in Berlin. Leonardo's one-man, one-work show aroused a great deal of interest and it provoked one of the few pieces of genuinely intelligent, immediately contemporary, criticism to have survived of a Renaissance work, by an agent of Isabella d'Este, Fra Pietro da Novellara:

> "Since he came to Florence he has done the drawing of a cartoon. He is portraying a Christ Child of about a year old who is almost slipping out of his Mother's arms to take hold of a lamb which he then appears to embrace. His Mother half rising from the lap of St Anne takes hold of the Child to separate him from the lamb (a sacrificial animal) signifying the Passion. St Anne, rising slightly from her sitting position, appears to want to restrain her daughter from separating the Child from the lamb. She is perhaps intended to represent the Church which would not have the Passion of Christ impeded." (Kemp-Walker 1989, p.273)

What we have in the design, according to Novellara, is a natural, human action - a mother withdrawing her child from something dangerous - which takes on symbolic resonance; a play between natural psychology and symbolic performance, in which enormous poignancy lies between the charm and delicacy of the action and the weight and pressure of the destiny. The subject of the Virgin and Child with St Anne is not an uncommon one, but it was usually presented iconically, without emotional or symbolic inflection. Only one earlier painting of the subject achieves Leonardo's level of subtlety, the *Sant'Anna Metterza* of Masaccio and Masolino. Here the roles are differently assigned. As the Child takes upon Himself the fullness of His destiny by His act of blessing, His mother, whilst holding Him tightly, looks out impassively, with a Sibylline gaze, aware of His fate. In this case it is she who represents the Church, one of her standard symbolic roles, and one which Masaccio has stressed by borrowing for her form the imperiously impassive block of Giotto's *Ognissanti Madonna*. The human reaction is now borne by St Anne, who, seeing the Child's action, suddenly becomes aware of what her daughter has always known. She raises her left hand in a gesture which combines surprise with an instinctive movement to shield and protect her divine grandchild - movement because we can see her sleeve swinging out to her

---

[3]    In my opinion Verrocchio's *David,* whose structure derives, of course, from Donatello's *St George,* should be dated in the first half of the 1460s.

left; her right hand she places on her daughter's shoulder in a gesture of comfort, one of her functions as defined by the inscription in her halo "Santa Anna e di nostra donna fast(igio)": St Anne is the supporter of the Virgin. The painting, whose central group was certainly designed by Masaccio, was looked at carefully by many artists later in the quattrocento, but only Leonardo perceived its full wealth of meaning and was able to rewrite it for his own purposes.

Leonardo's lost cartoon as recorded by Brescianino shows no visual relation to Masaccio's painting; his is purely a conceptual adaptation. But the painting's most dramatic visual feature, St Anne's tellingly foreshortened hand, was a motif that had the strongest appeal for Leonardo in other contexts: it is the central gesture of both versions of the *Virgin of the Rocks* (figs. 23-24). In the Louvre painting its effect is somewhat blunted by the outstretched pointing hand of the angel; in the London version the angel's hand is omitted, so the Virgin's gesture acquires greater prominence. And her other hand is also used in a way reminiscent of Masaccio's painting, but here to draw the adoring St John into the family group.

It seems likely that the foreshortened hand in Masaccio's painting was inspired by Donatello, specifically the gable relief of God the Father (Janson 1963, pl.11b) above the *St George* on Orsanmichele. Leonardo may well have recognised this, for he was himself deeply interested in Donatello. This I think, can be seen in the Louvre version of the *Virgin, Child, St Anne and a Lamb* (fig.29), a more rhythmical development of the 1501 cartoon, certainly begun before 1505 when it was reflected in Raphael's *Madonna of the Meadow* in Vienna. In the Louvre painting the sculptural three-dimensionality of the 1501 cartoon is reduced, the composition flattening out towards the front plane. Paradoxically, it is this very flattening which is due to a sculptural precedent - Donatello's relief of the *Virgin of the Clouds* (Janson 1963, pl.36) in the Museum of Fine Arts, Boston. The Virgin's diagonal movement across the surface, her extended leg and arms, the fall of drapery over her hip (where Freud found the vulture's head), her bare foot partially protruding from the drapery - these details surely prove the derivation.[4] Donatello's relief, incidentally, was a subject of interest at this moment, and Fra Bartolommeo had recently made a painted tabernacle for it.

If Leonardo looked to Donatello for a form in the Louvre painting, adding a reference to clarify and enrich a composition that presumably did not satisfy him in its first edition, he looked, I think, to another sculpture in his third version of the subject, the *Virgin, Child, St Anne and St John* cartoon in the National Gallery (fig.28). This shows a much more sculptural grouping,

---

[4] I have made this connection in lectures for a number of years; shortly after giving the present one I acquired the late Lord Clark's copy of H.W. Janson's *The Sculpture of Donatello* and was pleased to find the following annotation "Quincey Shaw *Madonna*; note connection of drapery with Leonardo and Raphael (also V. & A. Desiderio)".

reversing the emphasis of the Louvre painting. The figures form a powerful, but gracefully moving block, with the Virgin weighted to the left but carrying attention over to the right by her slowly spiralling movement, as she raises the Child to bestow His divine blessing and human affection on the tentatively advancing Giovannino - a remarkable invention. But the pose of the Virgin here too was surely inspired by an early quattrocento sculpture, another gable relief, the *Assumption of the Virgin* by Nanni di Banco above the Porta della Mandorla of Sta Maria del Fiore, where the Virgin in mid-ascension regally turns to bestow the girdle upon St Thomas.

The London Cartoon is now usually dated towards the end of Leonardo's second Florentine period, around 1508. At this time he was actively involved in a sculptural project, designing the group of *St John the Baptist between a Levite and a Pharisee* (Pope-Hennessy 1963, fig.39) which was executed by Gianfrancesco Rustici to stand above the north door of the Baptistery. Here Leonardo shows a powerful response to his most dangerous rival, Michelangelo - the links between Michelangelo's *St Matthew* (Pope-Hennessy 1963, fig.9), one of a series of twelve apostles intended for the Cathedral, and both the Levite and Pharisee are surely too close for coincidence (and Michelangelo in part returned the compliment in his *Moses*). But to Rustici's assistant, the young and ambitious sculptor Baccio Bandinelli, Leonardo strongly recommended the study of Donatello, advice that Bandinelli followed since he copied Donatello's works in several surviving drawings. In another extraordinarily elaborate drawing whose present whereabouts are unknown, Bandinelli also provides us with the most beautiful surviving record of a composition that Leonardo devised and probably painted at about this time, the half-length figure of the Annunciate Gabriel (**Plate 4**). Another copy, a much weaker painted one, is in the Öffentliche Kunstsammlung, Basle. We can get some idea of the quality of the original by a glance at Leonardo's Louvre *St John the Baptist* (**fig.33**), which shows a very similar composition; and Bandinelli's drawing suggests a painting of the highest finish.

One's first reaction on looking at such a figure is that it is radically new, that it dramatises the event in a hitherto unheard-of way, asking the spectator to imagine the reaction of the Virgin, to place him or herself in the Virgin's role. It seems to anticipate the drama of the relation between the work and the spectator so elaborately exploited in the 17th century, and even the shocks of 3-D cinema. But in this apparently epoch-making painting Leonardo was in fact responding to the invention of an earlier artist, Antonello da Messina, who painted at least two versions of the *Virgin Annunciate* (one now in the Munich Gemäldgalerie, the other in the Galleria Nazionale, Palermo) as though seen from the viewpoint of Gabriel. In producing his painting Leonardo was essentially creating a pendant to Antonello, more probably the second version which he may have seen in Venice, in 1500.

Antonello's work was certainly known in Milan when Leonardo was working there; indeed, Antonello had worked in Venice in 1474-5 and had actually been invited to Milan during this period. It seems likely that portraits by him were seen by Leonardo who responded to them quickly. Antonello's portraiture combined the Flemish bust-behind-parapet formula with a geometricality inspired by Piero della Francesca; and the regularisation of head and features in a painting like the so-called *Belle Ferronière* in the Louvre (Goldscheider 1943, pl.IIIa), which must be substantially by Leonardo's own hand, surely reflects Antonello's synthesis. Leonardo's range, of course was much wider than that of Antonello, but he would have been particularly open to respond to Antonello because Antonello's enterprise was to a considerable extent the same as his own. Leonardo's central objective, the guiding principle of his whole career, was precisely the combination of italianate physical structure and psychological drama with the universalising epidermis of Flemish painting, and before Leonardo it was this harmony that Antonello, albeit statically, supremely realised.

Rather as Tintoretto would later claim that the ideal painter should combine the drawing of Michelangelo with the colour of Titian, Leonardo might have claimed that one should combine the colour and texture of Van Eyck with the forms of Verrocchio, and his deep indebtedness to his master is not in doubt. Vasari pointed to the connection between Verrocchio's head studies and those of Leonardo; and the black chalk drawing of a woman's head by Verrocchio in the British Museum (Passavant 1969, pl.94) represents one of the unsurpassed peaks of Renaissance draughtsmanship. Its relation to Leonardo's drawings for the head of his *Leda* (58), made some thirty years later, is as clear to us as it was to Vasari. A link closer in time is provided by Verrocchio's tiny *Dreyfus Madonna* (Passavant 1969, pl.App.42) in the National Gallery of Art, Washington - which probably shows Flemish presence in the background landscape - for which a beautiful drawing by Verrocchio exists in Dresden. This painting both anticipates Leonardo's rich surface textures and subtlety of transitions, and also provided the armature for Leonardo's Munich *Virgin and Child with a Vase of Flowers* (fig.19) as well as the model for much of the detail. But in the grossly overfed Child, probably studied from repellent life, Leonardo was probably looking to a Roman sculpture of a child long familiar in Florence for the basic pose.

In another early painting, perhaps the earliest surviving by Leonardo, the Uffizi *Annunciation* (fig.21), we can see a similar combination: the angel is similar in type and characterisation to Antonio Rossellino's in the Chapel of the Cardinal of Portugal, while the landscape is unthinkable without some Eyckian source. Here, though, the elements remain relatively discrete. In the *Ginevra de'Benci* in Washington (fig.22) the integration is more complete. The portrait, which originally included the hands (as Lorenzo di Credi's adaptation of it in the Metropolitan Museum shows), is patently derived from - and is perhaps even of the same sitter as - Verrocchio's bust of *Flora* in the Bargello (Pope-Hennessy 1971, pl.77). But the subaqueous characterisation, the reptilian eyelids and the fragile modelling, surely reflect a model by Van Eyck's greatest pupil, Petrus Christus, perhaps the Berlin *Portrait of a Lady;* while the setting is based on the more prosaic art of Memling, of whom Verrocchio too was well aware.[5]

Other instances take us a little further, and show us that Leonardo's gaze was not fixed unanalytically on his master's work, but that he was also subtly cognizant of Verrocchio's own mentors. For the angel he painted in the still very mysterious *Baptism of Christ* in the Uffizi **(fig.20)**, he was surely looking back to an artist who had been a considerable influence on Verrocchio, Filippo Lippi, specifically to the kneeling Saint Frediano at the left of the Virgin in the Barbadori Altarpiece, now in the Louvre, whose twisting pose provides the most complete precedent for Leonardo's figure - one in which, incidentally, Leonardo also alluded to the Magdalen in Rogier van der Weyden's Uffizi *Entombment*. In the **Benois Madonna** in Leningrad **(fig.18)** - whose overpainted background has deprived us of another Flemish-inspired landscape view - Leonardo's lively three-quarter length arrangement is ultimately a grandchild of a type much used by Donatello, for example his gold-painted terracotta *Virgin and Child* in the Victoria and Albert Museum. Reliefs such as this had a considerable effect on Filippo Lippi who developed Donatello's structures in paintings like the Uffizi *Virgin and Child with Angels* which also anticipates Leonardo's richness of detailing of costume and elaborate landscape. The **Benois Madonna** is one of the few paintings by Leonardo prior to the Uffizi *Adoration* for which a preparatory drawing survives, in the British Museum **(fig.36)**; and this demonstrates what we might have surmised but could not otherwise have proved, that for his initial inspiration he looked to a famous prototype well known to you all, either one of the copies, with a round top, of which a fine example is in the Victoria and Albert Museum, or the sublime original, in the same museum, of Desiderio's *Dudley Madonna*. Leonardo has brought the cameo flatness of Desiderio's relief into the third dimension by twisting outwards the Virgin's head, but the derivation is unmistakable. Indeed, Leonardo may have recommended Bandinelli to study it, for several drawings of it by Bandinelli exist including, once more, an example in the Victoria and Albert Museum.

Desiderio, as well as adopting Donatello's *rilievo schiacciato* technique, was, of course, developing a type pioneered by Donatello in works such as the *Pazzi Madonna* in Berlin (probably of c.1422; Janson 1963, pl.19b), or a roughly contemporary design recorded in a terracotta in the Victoria and Albert Museum and various versions in marble, among them a recently-published example in Yerevan. In this relief, however, Donatello himself was looking back to an earlier prototype: the closeness of Donatello's group to Ambrogio Lorenzetti's *Virgin and Child* in Washington seems to me obvious.

---

[5] L. Campbell, "Memling and the followers of Verrocchio", *Burlington Magazine* CXXV, 1983, pp.675-6; and Hills, op.cit. in n.2.

And while the passage I quoted at the beginning makes it sound as though Leonardo was uninterested in trecento painting, I think that the juxtaposition of the **Madonna Litta** of the early 1480s (Goldscheider 1943, pl.67), probably autograph only in part, and Ambrogio Lorenzetti's famous *Madonna del Latte* (Siena, Seminario) speaks for itself; it seems to me impossible that Leonardo should not have known it.

This train of visual thought started with Desiderio, who was also the subtlest of portraitists. His *Bust of a Child* in the National Gallery of Art, Washington, was at one time attributed to Leonardo, and it was certainly with a model of this type in mind that Leonardo made a drawing for a similar bust in the 1490s (**30**). And the sense of vitality and wit that Desiderio infused into the usually rather stolid formula of the portrait bust (as, for example, in his so-called *Marietta Strozzi* in Berlin) was surely appreciated by Leonardo, who developed this idea to an extreme in the heavily narrativised **Cecilia Gallerani** (**fig.26**), which either follows, or was repeated in, a drawing for a panel of the *Magdalen* (Popham 1946, pl.29A), in the Princes Gate Collection at the Courtauld Institute.[6]

I would like to conclude my discussion by looking at two of Leonardo's grandest and most ambitious projects, one unfinished, the other barely started and soon lost - the **Adoration of the Magi** of around 1481-2 (**fig.16**) and the **Battle of Anghiari** of 1504-5 (cf. **fig.32**). The first is always taken as one of the foundations of High Renaissance art, a prototype of grandiloquent and vital forms organised in a clear geometrical way so that the painting presents an abstractly powerful formal arrangement within which the individual figures play their roles. In broad terms this is surely true. But Leonardo was not just a lonely pioneer. To a considerable extent he was taking up a theme recently not merely adumbrated, but brought to a high level of realisation, by Botticelli, in the National Gallery *Adoration* tondo and (more significantly for Leonardo) in his Uffizi *Adoration of the Magi*. Indeed, the rigorously perspectival background in one of Leonardo's preliminary drawings surely shows a desire to outdo Botticelli's perspective constructions of this period - an idea Leonardo dropped in the final design, where there is a dislocation between foreground and background, and a cavalier play with figure scales. But in its basic geometricality, the painting once more looks back beyond Botticelli, to the reliefs of the presiding genius of the first half of the quattrocento (and one of Botticelli's own sources), especially Donatello's amazing *Ascension and Delivery of the Keys* (Victoria and Albert Museum; Janson 1963, pl.39a). As well as creating a clear ground plan from a low-angle view and with an absolute exclusion of orthogonal indicators, here

---

[6]    The drawing has been dated both c.1480 and after 1500; I think it has passed unnoticed that the bowl-carrying nymph in Giovanni Bellini's Washington *Feast of the Gods* derives from this design.

Donatello achieves with apparent effortlessness that High Renaissance formula of a circle sealed by a pyramid.

In the *Battle of Anghiari*, Leonardo faced competition from a young man who had already shown himself to be a draughtsman of incomparable power, and whose status as the greatest of all heroic artists must already have been threateningly apparent - Michelangelo. The intended arrangement of the two Battle scenes - whether the frescoes were to be on opposite walls or on the same wall - is still in dispute. If the latter, comparison between the two artists would have been immediate and inescapable. I believe that a drawing in a private collection (**Plate 5**), fuller than other known copies but still very incomplete, is a genuine record of Leonardo's *Anghiari*. In addition to the amazing central group of horsemen, this shows figures of very great substance on either side, inventions indeed worthy of Michelangelo himself, and worthy to stand against him.[7] Leonardo had clearly put in a lot of thought.

As a whole, of course, this design with its very strong foreground emphasis (much more so than imagined by earlier reconstructions, mostly based on Leonardo's preparatory studies) clearly employs a relief arrangement, piling forms up the picture surface, to present a powerful hedge of figures. Here, surely, Leonardo was looking to antique reliefs, and to their imitations, such as the famous bronze battle relief by Bertoldo di Giovanni (Pope-Hennessy 1971, fig.139) now in the Bargello, which Leonardo would have known well in the Medici palace. This type provided Leonardo with the overall pattern. For the subsidiary figures Leonardo also turned to antique, and antiquising groups. In the background on the left he showed a soldier restraining the terrified horse of the fallen general - an obvious but very inventive adaptation of the antique 'Horse tamer' type, inspired either directly by the original or by Bertoldo's own splendid adaptation, the *Bellerophon* now in Vienna. In exercising his imagination in this artistic gymnasium, Leonardo was repeating, from a position of infinitely greater experience and sophistication - if not of genius - exactly the same training programme that his ferocious young rival had undergone nearly fifteen years before, brought up as he was on the antique, and on the antiquising work of Bertoldo, his sculptural master. And in the figure of the general sprawling in the foreground, Leonardo produced a brilliantly original adaptation of an antique river god, probably the so-called *Marforio*; a figure which is in some ways more satisfying than the reclining figure that Michelangelo devised for the right-hand side of the *Battle of Cascina*. Leonardo's invention greatly appealed to Raphael (who used it for the fallen Ananias in his tapestry cartoon and for Heliodorus in his *Expulsion*) and to Beccafumi (who adapted it on at least two occasions, in a famous

---

[7] I have argued at some length that this drawing is a 17th-century derivation from a lost design of Leonardo in "Leonardo da Vinci, Peter Paul Rubens, Pierre Nolasque Bergeret and the Fight for the Standard", *Achademia Leonardi Vinci*, I, 1988, pp.76-86.

drawing of *Two Nudes* in a private collection and in the *Moses and the Tables of the Law* designed for the pavement of Siena Cathedral). Indeed, Leonardo's figure was so Michelangelesque that Michelangelo himself appropriated it forty years later when he painted the *Conversion of Saul* (Vatican, Cappella Paolina).

To consider a relation like this, where Leonardo is more Michelangelesque than Michelangelo, makes us realise the extent to which a style that we might be tempted to think of as innate and involuntary can be the product of intention and selection. I hope that in pointing to some of his visual sources (and there are many others) I have helped remove Leonardo from the position of *sui generis* artistic isolation in which he is customarily found, and to replace him in an artistic stream in which his extraordinary intelligence found sustenance, and which, in return, he deepened and enlarged.

Paul Joannides

# Leonardo's techniques

I do not have any radical ideas or original discoveries to offer in this lecture about Leonardo's techniques. Many of his paintings are direly in need of conservation, which could provide the opportunity for thorough scientific investigation of the media and pigments he used, and how he built up the paint layer by layer. But until this is done, we will have little new information beyond that which is coming out of the current restoration of the *Last Supper* (**fig.25**). What I wish to do, therefore, is to emphasise some general points made in other lectures about Leonardo's extraordinary inventiveness, and to see how this quality is shown both in the new ways he used known techniques, and in the new techniques he evolved to help him to solve the new artistic problems that he set himself.

This lecture falls into three sections, considering first Leonardo's plans for casting the *Sforza Horse*, in which we can see both his inventiveness and his thorough research and planning. Secondly, we will look at some of his drawing techniques, and thirdly at the development of his painting techniques with special reference to his growing concern with problems of tonality and tonal unification. The second and third sections run fairly well together, because some of the suggestions to be made about the drawings will have some bearing on his paintings and painting techniques.

After a long catalogue of his abilities as a military and civil engineer, Leonardo wrote in his celebrated letter of about 1482 to Lodovico Sforza in Milan:

> "Also I can execute sculpture in marble, bronze and clay. Likewise in painting, I can do everything possible as well as any other, whosoever he may be. Moreover, work could be undertaken on the bronze horse which will be to the immortal glory and eternal honour of the auspicious memory of His Lordship your father, and of the illustrious house of Sforza..." (Kemp/Walker 1989, pp.252-3)

In the initial plan the horse was to have been life-size; but by the late 1480s it was conceived as being colossal - four times life-size. On 22 July 1489 the Florentine ambassador in Milan wrote to Lorenzo 'il Magnifico' de'Medici:

> "The Duke Lodovico is planning to erect a worthy monument to his father, and in accordance with his orders Leonardo has been asked to make a model in the form of a large horse, to be cast in bronze, ridden by the Duke Francesco in full armour. As his Highness has in mind something wonderful, the like of which has never been seen, he has directed me to write to you and ask if

you will kindly send him one or two Florentine artists who specialise in this kind of work. For, although the Duke has given the commission to Leonardo, it seems to me that he is not confident that he will succeed." (Goldscheider 1943, p.34)

However, Leonardo evidently retained the commission, since he wrote: "On the 23rd of April 1490... I started the horse afresh" (MS C, f.15v); and in a memorandum in Codex Madrid II, f.157v (cf. **115**) he wrote: "In the evening, May 17, 1491. Here a record shall be kept of everything related to the bronze horse presently under execution." (Reti ed. 1974, p.87). By this date, the full-size model was complete. The sources are not precise as to the material of this model: Matteo Bandello described it as an 'earthen Horse', Paolo Giovio as 'a colossus in clay', and Paolo Cortese as 'a clayey horse'. In Codex Madrid II Leonardo himself called it the 'earthen horse', but it might perhaps have been made of the 'moulding stucco' mentioned in the Codex Atlanticus. Making an earthen or stucco model, however, implies rejection of the lost-wax method of casting in which the final model layer to be cast is of wax over a core of refractory clay. The material from which Leonardo made his model would not have been able to stand up to the heat and pressure of casting, and would have disintegrated. In the lost-wax technique the original is lost in the process, so is not available for detailed comparison when the sculptor is working on the cast. Moreover, it is impossible to obtain a homogeneous thickness of the modelled wax. If the wax is not uniformly thick, the thickness of the bronze of the cast cannot be controlled. Thus there is no way of calculating how much bronze is required for the casting.[1]

In the case of the *Sforza Horse* it was absolutely necessary to keep the weight as low as possible; therefore the layer of cast bronze had to be as thin as possible. Once the full-size model had been built, in the old courtyard of the castle where it was intended that the monument should finally be erected, Leonardo made a piece-mould from which the final cast could more precisely and accurately be made. This technique was untested at the date. Even in 1504 Pomponius Gauricus in his treatise *De Scultura* does not refer to it; and the first extensive discussion of piece-mould casting comes in Cellini's *Treatise on Goldsmithing and Sculpture*, first published in 1568. Of his piece-mould for the horse Leonardo wrote:

"You should prepare a form of three parts for each roundness of any of the limbs; it will be much easier to detach it from the earthen horse" (Codex Madrid II, f.148r; Reti ed. 1974, p.96);

---

[1] For the casting technique of the *Sforza Horse*, see M.V. Brugnoli, "Il Cavallo", in Reti ed. 1974, pp.86-109.

and this is clearly illustrated in the red chalk drawing in Codex Madrid II (in which notebook he made extensive notes about his new developments in casting techniques) for the piece-mould for the horse's head (115). Pieces were built up over the greased model; they were then detached, dried, and reassembled to make the 'female' mould. Within this, a layer of even thickness of wax or potter's clay (for Cellini later, the *lasagna*) was laid: from the weight of substance used the weight of bronze needed for casting could be calculated. Within this again, the male 'mould' was made from refractory clay, a heat-resistant material which can withstand baking and contact with the molten bronze.

Drawings of the 1480s indicate that Leonardo had been experimenting with this new casting process while working on the earlier *Sforza Monument* design, which had a life-size, rearing horse. The 'female' mould could also be used to cast a wax countermodel which could be checked against the original model to see if there were deficiencies in the piece-mould. Later notes written by Leonardo show that this was certainly to have been a stage in the casting of the *Trivulzio Monument* in the middle of the first decade of the 16th century.

Another series of studies in Codex Madrid II (f.149v) shows the casting pit that Leonardo was to have used (Reti ed. 1974, pl.107/1). The view from above shows the assembled outer mould flanked by multiple furnaces, of the type he had designed for casting cannon, in which the bronze would have been melted before pouring. Below, Leonardo wrote:

"This is how the horse shall be cast, but provide that the neck first be filled up with its bronze by means of many spouts until line m-n is reached. At this point all the other spouts must be unplugged at once" (Reti ed. 1974, p.107)

The Codex Madrid II section on the horse is almost entirely concerned with the problems of casting: it provides explicit explanations of the processes of model building, the preparation of the piece mould, casting the countermodel, preparing the casting pits and ovens, and finally casting the colossal statue. Leonardo's whole process, demonstrated graphically and in detailed verbal description, provides extraordinarily inventive solutions to the huge and complex problems that casting this colossal horse would have posed. One may doubt if even Leonardo could have pulled off this feat; but it cannot be doubted that his profound thinking and experimentation about the difficulties, in terms both of engineering and of bronze-casting, established him as the only sculptor of the time remotely capable of attempting it.

The Hayward Gallery exhibition showed Leonardo's brilliant inventiveness also as a draughtsman. One of the most remarkable, and perhaps least expected, impressions that the visitor took away from the exhibition was of the great range of colour of Leonardo's drawings. This is in part due to the different techniques, and different combination of techniques, that he used when investigating different problems; and in part due to the range of types and preparations of the paper he used. This discussion will start with some consideration of the surfaces that Leonardo drew on.

Early in his career, Leonardo predictably took up and exploited to sophisticated effect a standard technique of the Verrocchio workshop for the study of drapery folds. This procedure is described by Vasari in the *Life of Leonardo da Vinci*:

> "Sometimes he made clay models, draping the figures with rags dipped in plaster, and then drawing them painstakingly on fine Rheims cloth or prepared linen. These drawings were done in black and white with the point of the brush, and the results were marvellous..." (Vasari/Bull 1971, p.256)

Although probably not even Verrocchio's invention, since Vasari writes of Piero della Francesca experimenting with the technique, this technique had the obvious virtue of allowing as much time as the draughtsman could need for making the study, since once the plaster had set the drapery model studied would be unchanging. One such 'cast-drapery' study (3) shows clearly the weave of the linen, and the careful application of water-based pigment and white heightening over a slightly greenish-grey preparation. This study, which can be indirectly associated with the drapery of the kneeling angel that Leonardo painted in the Verrocchio workshop *Baptism of Christ* (**fig.20**), shows the clarity with which Leonardo observed both the morphology of the drapery folds generated by the structure of the forms beneath, and the effect of the play of light indicating the texture of the fabric.

Aside from the group of drapery studies on linen, Leonardo's drawings were virtually all made on paper. However, he used a wider variety of papers than any other draughtsman of his time. The standard type of paper can be seen in many drawings: the sheets of studies of cats (38) or of horses (72), to take examples more or less at random, show the characteristic surface texture and light grey-cream colour. In certain circumstances Leonardo used other papers, for instance the thick, coarsely manufactured grey paper which supplies a marvellously rugged expressive strength to reinforce the highly individualised head of an old man (36) drawn late in his career. In a group of late anatomical studies (19, 55, 119) Leonardo used a notebook made up of large sheets of the blue paper known as *carta azzurra*, which was imported from the Middle East and much used by Venetian draughtsmen.

Like all other 15th-century draughtsmen, Leonardo prepared his paper with a pigmented surface for drawing in silverpoint: the colours vary, but that he seems to have liked a blue preparation (8, 40, 67) may explain his later use of *carta azzurra*. The coloured preparation for silverpoint drawing provided a middle tone between the subtle greenish-grey of the silverpoint line and the

35

white pigment heightening, and thus increased the tonal range of the silverpoint draughtsman. When studying other motifs, Leonardo used warmer colours for his preparation: a delicate buff for the study of hands (4) generally associated with the portrait of *Ginevra de'Benci* (fig.22), or a light pink for the head of a bear (37) and the companion sheet of studies of a wolf's paw (39).

It may have been the quality of colouristic warmth inherent in this ground that led Leonardo sometimes to coat paper with a reddish preparation before drawing in chalk. This would seem especially appropriate for studies of human form (such as 15, in which Leonardo drew in pen and ink over red chalk in studies of legs), but was also used in pure nature-study drawings of plants (28, 44). Through the use of what might be called 'red-on-red' the red chalk lines and tonal gradients which define the plant forms emerge gently from the coloured environment which envelops them: the effect (and perhaps also the artistic intention) is similar to that obtained by Leonardo in the relationship of figures to atmosphere in his last major painting, the Paris *Virgin, Child, St Anne and a Lamb* (fig.29) which will be discussed later.

In another nature drawing, the early study of a lily (42) which is pricked presumably for transfer to a painting, Leonardo added not only a brown ink wash but also a light yellow watercolour as a coloured background for the flower. This unusual and inventive procedure sets the scene for the extensive use of coloured washes for diagrammatic purposes in a wide range of drawings. The principal internal organs and blood vessels in one of his earliest anatomical drawings (50) are picked out in a somewhat unappealing greenish colour; the whirling movements of the flow of water against and through a breakwater (62) are diagrammatically illustrated in dull green-grey and blue; and special features on maps - the river (blue) and land (green) of the Arno west of Florence (48), or the moat, open land, and buildings of Imola (98) - are identified by 'colour-coding' in watercolour. Finally, a further major innovation is the coloration added to the portrait drawing of *Isabella d'Este* (fig.27) in which, perhaps for the first time, Leonardo used pastel to pick out the pattern on the sitter's costume: one of the earliest drawings made as (and intended to be preserved as) a finished portrait, this set a pattern for colour in portrait-drawings followed in the 16th century by Holbein amongst others.

As for the drawing techniques themselves, Leonardo exploited the entire range from silverpoint to black chalk with greater versatility than any other draughtsman up to his time, or perhaps since. From his early crisp treatment of the clear, invariable silverpoint line which demands great patience in the construction of form through tonal hatching (2, 4), Leonardo developed towards an atmospheric, soft haziness of handling of black chalk (31, 79). His handling of the pen ranged inventively from the briefest of sketches of dynamic models (5, 7) through careful, diagrammatic drawing (25, 43) to highly sophisticated excavations of three-dimensional forms and spaces through variable hatching and cross-hatching (**9, 93**). But perhaps his greatest and historically most significant innovation in drawing technique was the introduction and full exploitation of red chalk. This is a more incisive material than black chalk, and in hands as skilled as Leonardo's could combine the sharp precision of the silverpoint line with the flexibility of the pen (as in **47, 73**). It can, moreover, combine these two qualities with both the richness of smooth, graded modelling across the full tonal range (**32, 33**) and the human character of the warm, flesh-toned colour. The archetypal example of Leonardo's brilliance as an expressive draughtsman is his exploration of sharp outline and strained, modelled musculature in his use of red chalk on red prepared paper in the great study for the head of Judas (**88**) for the *Last Supper*.

Recent work on restoration and scientific examination of the *Last Supper* (**fig.25**) has revealed two technical features unusual in late 15th-century wallpainting.[2] It is well known that Leonardo did not use the standard *buon fresco* technique, despite Cennino Cennini's view that "...to work on the wall... is the most agreeable and impressive kind of work", a view later echoed by Vasari, who wrote:

> "Of all the methods that painters employ, painting on the wall is the most masterly and beautiful, because it consists in doing in a single day that which, in the other methods, may be retouched day after day, over the work already done... There is needed a hand that is dexterous, resolute and rapid, but most of all a sound and perfect judgment... the painter... should have for his guide the very greatest experience, it being supremely difficult to bring fresco work to perfection... fresco is truly the most manly, most certain, most resolute and durable of all methods of wallpainting..."[3]

There are three principal reasons why Leonardo could not use *buon fresco* for the *Last Supper*. First, he could not work at the speed required by fresco: this is made clear by Matteo Bandello's account of Leonardo's procedure, in his *Le Novelle* (Lucca, 1554):

---

[2] For further discussion of the technique of the *Last Supper*, and references to technical literature, see the lecture by Pietro Marani, on pp.45-52 below.

[3] Cennino Cennini, *The Craftsman's Handbook*, trans. D.V. Thompson Jr., New Haven 1933, p.42; G. Vasari *On Technique*, trans, L.S. Maclehose, London 1907, pp.221-2.

"He would often come to the convent at early dawn; and this I have seen him do myself. Hastily mounting the scaffolding, he worked diligently until the shades of evening compelled him to cease, never thinking to take food at all, so absorbed was he in his work. At other times he would remain there three or four days without touching his picture, only coming for a few hours to remain before it, with folded arms, gazing at his figures as if to criticise them himself. At midday too, when the glare of the sun at its zenith has made barren all the streets of Milan, I have seen him hasten from the citadel, where he was modelling his colossal horse, without seeking the shade, by the shortest way to the convent, where he would add a touch or two and immediately return." (Goldscheider 1943, pp.34-7)

Fresco demands that a day's patch is completed while the plaster is still wet. Work has to be rapid, and by implication the painter does not have a great deal of time for thought, and often needs to work to formulae or to conventional patterns. This is suggested by Cennini's recommendations on how to paint certain facial types which evidently did not, in his approach, need to be differentiated or individualised. This was not satisfactory for Leonardo, who needed to assert naturalistically calculated, individual expressive ideas through each figure.

Second, he had to be able to work up the whole surface together, whereas the standard sort of day-work pattern which we can see for instance in Ghirlandaio's *Last Supper* (Florence, Ognissanti) implies a piecemeal procedure by which he probably started at top left and worked across and down patch by patch. Vasari's description of the scaffolding for the *Battle of Anghiari* shows that Leonardo needed to devise a system which provided the greatest flexibility and allowed him to range all over the surface in the gradual definition of the whole composition:

"It is said that to draw the cartoon Leonardo constructed an ingenious scaffolding that he could raise or lower by drawing it together or extending it. He also conceived the wish to paint the picture in oils, but to do this he mixed such a thick composition for laying on the wall that, as he continued his painting in the hall, it started to run and spoil what had been done. So shortly afterwards he abandoned the work." (Vasari/Bull 1971, p.268)

As the unfinished *Adoration of the Magi* (**fig.16**) shows, Leonardo was accustomed, and indeed demanded of his working method that it should be possible, to build up the picture as a whole, laying in the tonal underpaint all over the work before beginning on the top pigment surface. Given again what is said of his procedure in the Bandello account, he evidently had to be able to observe the whole, pulling it together in light and shade, and unifying it in colour as he proceeded. He could not afford the risks or difficulties of mismatched pigments from one day's work to the next, or any of the other problems posed by the *buon fresco* technique.

Finally, Leonardo had to work towards the deeper tonalities, in other words from light to dark as in oil-painting, in order to achieve the tonal unification that he demanded of himself, rather than building up the light tones to culminate in white highlights, as in tempera painting or *buon fresco*.

For all these reasons the *buon fresco* technique, however highly recommended by Cennino and later by Vasari, was completely unsuited to Leonardo's working methods and artistic aims. Hence his choice of a technique based on panel-painting in oils, the technique of easel painting which he had learned as early as his time in Verrocchio's workshop and which we know he used in the Paris *Virgin of the Rocks* (**fig.23**), since the confraternity documents of 1483 say over and over again that "everything is to be done in oil" (Kemp/Walker 1989, pp.268-70). But it is not in fact so much the unorthodox medium used for applying of the pigments to the wall that has caused the *Last Supper* to deteriorate as the unorthodox preparation of the surface for painting. Because Leonardo could not use *buon fresco*, he had to prepare the wall as though for panel painting; and he added a new feature to this preparation which seems to have caused the subsequent problems.

The preparation was made up essentially of three layers. The first was a layer of rough plaster, the normal plaster mortar without organic binders, such as was conventional for the *arriccio* layer in wall-painting. Second came a preparatory layer, 1-2 mm thick: this is the equivalent to the fresco *intonaco*, but it includes magnesium compounds as well as the usual calcium carbonate. It contains calcium carbonate, calcium hydroxide, magnesium hydroxide and, notably, nesquelonite, a crystalline magnesium carbonate ($MgCO_3.3H_2O$). These salts are bound and applied with a medium consisting of a drying oil, perhaps walnut oil, saponified oils, and a non-soluble protein, probably egg. The advantage to Leonardo of the make-up of this layer is that the magnesium carbonate increases the luminosity, and provides a more brilliant white ground for painting. Leonardo wrote:

"For those colours which you wish to be beautiful, always first prepare a pure white ground. I say this in relation to colours which are transparent..." (Kemp/Walker 1989, p.71)

It seems, then that he was preparing for the application of pigment to some extent at least in the form of transparent glazes, so that light would be reflected back through the glazes from the pure white ground, and the colours would thereby gain in brilliancy and resonance. The problem with this complex mixed ground, however, is that it has shrunk with age, cracking both on the surface and into its thickness. It is this cracking, apparently, and the consequent transmission of the damp drawn into the wall behind from the high watertable on which the church and refectory of Sta Maria delle Grazie are built, that has caused the decay and loss of the paint surface.

The third layer of the elaborate preparation of the wall was the priming layer, a thin layer of lead white, which filled in the pores and roughness of the preparatory layer and again enhances the colours by the strength of its whiteness. Lead white can not be exploited in any mural technique which uses water-bound pigments, because of atmospheric deterioration; its presence here therefore again implies that a binding medium, of walnut oil for instance, was to be used. Onto the priming layer, the pigments themselves were laid, using a mixed binding medium similar to that which Leonardo might have used for panel painting. Both walnut oil and non-soluble proteins, probably from egg-tempera, have been found in the paint layers: Leonardo may well have alternated layers of paint using egg-tempera and oil, according to the brightness and tonality of the colours used at each point. A sample taken from the red sleeve of Christ's robe had: 1.5 mm of carbon black underpaint, 0.4 mm of vermilion, and 0.2 mm of red lake glaze. Leonardo was concerned here to give maximum effect to the red pigment by laying it on a layer of black underpaint. Some colours needed to be enhanced by the magnesium and lead whites; vermilion needed to be toned down with the black foundation. Tonal modelling was achieved by using thin layers of the semi-transparent red lake glaze. Like lead white, vermilion is scarcely ever used in *buon fresco*: here the binder protects it from atmospheric deterioration.

What we find in the handling of red lake glaze in the *Last Supper* conforms with Leonardo's own words:

> "It must be noted in what situation the same colour looks most beautiful in nature... black possesses beauty in shadow, and white in light, and blue and green and tawny in middle shadow, and yellow and red in light, and gold in reflected light, and lake in middle shadow." (Kemp/Walker 1989, p.72)

Lake glazes are thus best used for darkening into a half-shadow, as in the modelling on Christ's robe, where the lake-glazed vermilion reaches its highest intensity, or 'beauty' as Leonardo expresses it. Of the principle of glazing, he further wrote:

> "When a transparent colour lies over another colour differing from it, a compound colour is composed which differs from each of the simple colours from which it is compounded. This is seen in the smoke coming out of chimneys, which when seen against the blackness of the chimney makes a blue colour, and when it rises to be seen against the blue of the air appears grey or

reddish. Similarly, purple placed over blue makes the colour of violet... and brightness above darkness makes a blue which will be of greater beauty to the extent that the brightness and darkness are most intense." (Kemp/Walker 1989, p.71)

Leonardo fully realised the potential of glazing as a technical means towards achieving intensity of colour and breadth of tonal range. And it is singularly appropriate that Leonardo should have used the example of smoke in these observations about the changes that can be made through the application of translucent pigmented layers, since in the experiments undertaken in his latest paintings he worked towards generating a misty atmospheric 'smokiness' which would tonally embrace his figures and unify them with the tonality of their environment.

This is why Leonardo aimed to provide his figures with a context in which a unity can be achieved between colour and tonality.[4] The ultimate success, as we will see, was in the Louvre *Virgin, Child, St Anne and a Lamb* (**fig.28**), where the unifying tonality is that of the open air; earlier steps towards this were made using enclosed settings so that the lighting can be carefully controlled, and the tonal range deepened into heavy shadows. In the *Benois Madonna* (**fig.18**) Leonardo constructed a containing but deliberately ill-defined interior setting around the Virgin and Child: the illumination is focused, and the broad tonal gradient generated allows Leonardo to model full, physically intermeshed forms into a securely three-dimensional group by glazing his colours down from their greatest intensity into deep shadow. The major forerunner of Leonardo who exploited the enclosing setting for these purposes was Jan van Eyck: and this is significant because in various ways Leonardo's technical handling appears to owe as much to his understanding of van Eyck's means and intentions as to any other source of knowledge about oil-painting techniques. Van Eyck's exploration of the recesses of shadow in the interior, and of the enriching of tonality in the shadows of drapery folds, for example, is a remarkable precedent for Leonardo's method of limiting the light and thus generating a strong plasticity, however different the results may look.

These were Leonardo's pictorial preoccupations in the 1480s, at the time of work on the first version of the *Virgin of the Rocks* (**fig.23**). Here, his primary aim was to achieve consistency of tone; and this implied the need both to develop a greater intensity of colour and to limit the lighting to a single direction and strength. So he set the figure group against a darkened background, although not actually within a rocky grotto such as that

---

[4] The major stimulus for this discussion was J. Shearman, "Leonardo's Colour and Chiaroscuro", *Zeitschrift für Kunstgeschichte* XXV, 1962, pp.13-47

constructed later for the setting of the London version (**fig.24**). Whereas in the National Gallery painting the setting entirely contains the figures, here the sky is visible above the figures, and the rocks serve as a deep-coloured foil to the group. The figures are fairly strongly lit by a focused light, and a firm plasticity is again developed by deepening the shadows. And yet, internal reflections counteract too much Leonardo's efforts to achieve fully rounded forms, and the precise lines of the silhouettes on the shaded sides of the figures, where the forms do not smoothly merge with the atmospheric shadow of the setting, detach the figures from their context, and stress the impression that this is a high relief group set against a rocky backdrop. In the later version, the figure-group is integrated more fully within the grotto setting, and the keen, focused light selects out forms which are important to the expressive meaning of the figures' interrelationships and leaves other forms to merge fully with the embracing penumbra.

A comparison of the head of the angel in the Paris version (**fig.23**) with the head of the angel in the Uffizi *Annunciation* (**fig.21**) painted a decade or so earlier shows that the *Virgin of the Rocks* head is more fully structured through smooth modelling and glazing, in contrast with the rather bland, low-relief form which is flatly silhouetted against the distant trees, and which, illuminated by a generalised light, lacks the three-dimensionality of tonal modelling. Once more using a van Eyck comparison, the head of *Eve* from the Ghent Altarpiece, one can sense that between these two works Leonardo was evolving in an Eyckian direction in his use of glazes to enrich the tonal resonance of shadow and modelled form. Predictably, perhaps, at this still relatively early stage of his Milanese career, Leonardo used silverpoint to study this angel's head (Turin, Royal Library 15572; Popham 1946, pl.157), building up the tonal range across cheek and jaw in his typically precise and systematic way, and using immaculately fine hatching strokes. But this purely graphic technique of parallel hatching can in no sense provide an equivalent to the soft modulations of tone which Leonardo achieved with his oil glazes in the painting. Although it captures beautifully the delicacy, and to a degree the textural sensitivity, of the head, silverpoint is ultimately too limited, too specifically linear a drawing technique to provide Leonardo with the means he needed for exploring the tonal unification which had increasingly become his main pictorial preoccupation by the time he worked on the London version of the composition.

Looking again at the same angel's head, in the National Gallery painting (**fig.24**), we see that colour has become submerged into tonal modulation: plasticity is achieved by the absolutely, unfalteringly smooth transition across the tonal gradient. This is perhaps the pictorial culmination of the researches on light and shade, and into the tonal character of shadows cast by focused lights, that Leonardo pursued in the early 1490s, and which are epitomised in his diagrammatic study of light and shade (**102**), where he hatched and washed in the range of shadows cast at different points. On this sheet

42

Leonardo wrote:

> "every shadow made by an opaque body smaller than the source of light casts derivative shadows tinged by the colour of their original shadows";

and further,

> "every light which falls perpendicularly on opaque bodies produces the first degree of brightness, and that surface will be darker which receives the light at more oblique angles..." (Catalogue 1989, p.182)

This second principle in particular lies behind the meticulous clarity of gradations of light and shade which we see in the modelling of the angel in the London *Virgin of the Rocks* (fig.24). We may hazard, I think, that the preliminary study for this head was drawn in red chalk, and might have looked in handling much like the study of the head of a young soldier for the *Battle of Anghiari* (Budapest, Museum of Fine Arts 344; Popham 1946, pl.199), or the study for the head of St James the Greater (**89**) drawn a few years before. The crisp precision of outline and the clarity of modelling right across the tonal gradient, which are ideally achievable with the combination of razor-sharp edge and warmly merging rubbed tone of the stick of red chalk, generate a softness of texture and a smooth roundness of form which parallel closely the fully evolved chiaroscuro modelling of the angel's face.

But if in the National Gallery painting the enclosed setting embraces the figures spatially more fully than in the earlier version of the *Virgin of the Rocks*, the strongly directional light creates some pictorial discontinuity because of the selective spotlighting, and this tends to disrupt atmospheric unification. In the late Paris *Virgin, Child, St Anne and a Lamb* (fig.28) Leonardo worked on this issue, by exploring the technical and colouristic means by which the figures can be atmospherically unified within an open-air environment, so that the stridency of illumination of the *Virgin of the Rocks* grotto context is modified down. A tonally uniform, faintly tinted neutral grey is used for the highlights on forms and draperies, in place of the higher-key brightness of tone on the *Virgin of the Rocks* highlights. Leonardo used colours which blend together in the middle tonal range, and lose intensity again in the deeper shadows: in other words, he concentrated his colour-scheme on those colours which, in the passage I quoted earlier, he had specified as having their greatest intensity in the half shadow - green, blue, tawny, and red lake glaze. But the shadows no longer have the resonating tonal depth of those of the National Gallery painting: they lack that dark opaqueness, and retain some colour, albeit subdued and repressed. Leonardo no longer needed to provide an artificial encompassing darkness, and in the absence of focused illumination the tonal range is much reduced, so that the figure group now harmonises tonally, colouristically and atmospherically with the surrounding air and with the distant landscape.

No wonder, then, that the head of St Anne (17) was studied in a grey-black chalk. Using this technique, with its tendency towards broader, less incisive line and its potential for developing hazy, soft tonalities and tonal modulations, Leonardo explored the forms of the head enveloped in a delicately toned *sfumato* atmosphere. His concern here is no longer with full plasticity generated by a full tonal range from bright highlight to deep shadow, but rather with exploring those half-lights and diffused shadows by which tonal unification of form in dull daytime light can be achieved. Thus in this culmination of Leonardo's exploration of technical means to investigate and solve problems of pictorial tonality, the containing atmosphere is at once more convincingly naturalistic and more expressively subtle.

Francis Ames-Lewis

# Leonardo's *Last Supper:* some problems of the restoration and new light on Leonardo's art

Before considering the present campaign of restoration of the *Last Supper* in the Refectory of Sta Maria delle Grazie, Milan (**fig. 25**), and showing the visual results of that restoration, I think it is first necessary to review briefly some general problems concerning the painting itself from the points of view both of its interpretation and of its chronology.[1] It is useful to recall that twelve or thirteen years before Leonardo began to paint the *Last Supper* he had already experimented with the problem of grouping a number of figures around a fulcrum (a crucial representational problem in the *Last Supper*) in the unfinished *Adoration of the Magi* in the Uffizi, Florence (**fig. 16**). This painting is, in my opinion, the starting point for any full understanding of the meaning of Leonardo's mural painting. Although usually considered as an early painting, the *Adoration* in fact reveals the mastery of Leonardo at the age of thirty. It is fully a work of art, one indebted to the best traditions of Florentine sculpture, as Luisa Becherucci has pointed out,[2] with direct quotations from Ghiberti, Donatello and, we may add, from Verrocchio's group of *Christ and St Thomas* (Florence, Orsanmichele).[3] In the Uffizi *Adoration*, a translation into painting of Alberti's theory of *istoria*, the animation of the figures is generated by the vision of the Virgin with the Child; hence the painting is the record of the emotions and reactions of the figures set around the central group. In the same way, in the *Last Supper* Christ's words "One of you shall betray me" strike the apostles like sound waves, rebounding from one to another and creating the variety of their poses, gestures and movements. It is as though diagrams of laws of acoustics, optics and dynamics had been directly translated into painting. I have already noted that the different reactions of the apostles correspond to the different ways a light ray is reflected and returns, according to the type of surface refracting

---

[1] I would like to express my gratitude to the Leonardo da Vinci Society and to the Istituto Italiano di Cultura, London, for the opportunity they have given me to show in London the progress of the current restoration of the *Last Supper*. Thanks are due also to Professor Martin Kemp, to Drs Francis Ames-Lewis and Richard Schofield for their assistance, and to Professor Sandro Vaciago for his hospitality.

[2] See L. Becherucci, "L'Adorazione dei Magi" (1977) in *Leonardo. La pittura*, Amplified Edition with an Introduction by P.C. Marani, Florence 1985, pp. 39-48.

[3] See my paper "Tracce ed elementi verrocchieschi nella tarda produzione grafica e pittorica di Leonardo", presented to the conference *Andrea del Verrocchio and his Position in late Quattrocento Art: A re-evaluation 500 years after His Death*, Harvard University Center for Italian Renaissance Studies, Villa I Tatti, Florence, 16 June 1989 (publication forthcoming).

it.[4] In approaching the *Last Supper* therefore, we should also consider the related studies in optics, mechanics and dynamics which occupied Leonardo in the immediately preceding period and during the years he was working on the painting.

At the same time, Leonardo undoubtedly intended to offer a very broad compendium of the 'moti dell'anima', the 'movements of the soul' reflected in multiple attitudes and human expressions, as he partially did (without, however, the deep knowledge of the laws of dynamics and mechanics that he had gained by late on in the Milanese period) in the Uffizi *Adoration*. What other 'test', what words other than those pronounced by Christ could so well have illustrated Leonardo's artistic and scientific theories? In the 'Treatise on Painting' we can read for example that:

> "The movements of men are as varied as are the emotions which pass through their minds. And each emotion moves men more or less, depending on its greater or lesser force, and also on the age of the man, for in the same situation a young man will act otherwise than an old one." (McMahon 1956, I p.152)

Here the terminology and the mental process implied are exactly the same as those applied by Leonardo to the study of the causes of 'accidental' or induced movement in mechanics and dynamics. In this context the figure of Christ, the main actor in the story unfolding before us, must be seen as the 'Prime Mover', to use the term that Leonardo used later in his career, and to which Martin Kemp has recently drawn attention.[5]

I have underlined this dynamic interpretation of the *Last Supper* because I am not convinced that the scene shows the 'Institution of the Eucharist', and I am convinced that this doctrinal event cannot be taken as the key to understanding the painting.[6] The moment of the sacrament precedes the revelation of the betrayal, and certainly does not demand such an emotional

---

[4] P.C. Marani, *Leonardo's Last Supper*, Milan 1986, p.9ff. See also my "Leonardo dalla scienza all'arte: un cambiamento di stile, gli antefatti, una cronologia", in *Fra Rinascimento, Manierismo e Realtà. Scritti di Storia dell'arte in memoria di Anna Maria Brizio*, Florence 1984, p.44.

[5] See Kemp 1981, Chapter V.

[6] This thesis was revived by L. Steinberg, "Leonardo's Last Supper", *Art Quarterly*, XXXVI/4, 1973, pp.297-410. Ottino della Chiesa (1967), Brizio (1977) and others (included the present writer) have rejected that theory. In trying to demonstrate that the *Last Supper* symbolizes the institution of the Eucharist the recent M. Rossi - A. Rovetta, *Il Cenacolo di Leonardo. Cultura domenicana, iconografia eucaristica e tradizione lombarda*, "Quaderni del Restauro" 5, Milan 1988, attributed to Leonardo the knowledge of a lot of theological texts, in Latin, that he could never have read.

and dramatic reaction as we can see here in the poses and movements of the apostles. Moreover I do not believe that Leonardo would have agreed to illustrate simply a dogmatic concept suggested by the Dominican friars of Sta Maria delle Grazie. Leonardo wanted to leave to posterity the final manifestation of his programmatic artistic manifesto. To consider Leonardo as a mere illustrator of a theological idea without imposing his personal interpretation, is to fail to understand his mental attitudes to such an extent that I think it unnecessary to discuss this thesis any further.

Another issue I have recently reviewed in studies on the *Last Supper* is the problem of the chronology, paying special attention to establishing the moment at which Leonardo began to study the composition and, with reference to this, the chronology of his preparatory drawings. The scientific observations and theoretical notes on painting which relate directly to the *Last Supper* are from manuscripts datable between 1490 and 1494, and this seems to confirm that the preparatory studies were begun in about 1490-2. Moreover, insufficient attention is usually given to Matteo Bandello's testimony as evidence for dating the *Last Supper*. Speaking of how Leonardo often went to the Grazie to work on the mural, he refers to the equestrian monument to Francesco Sforza:

> "I have also seen him (when the caprice or whim took him) at midday when the sun is highest leave the Corte Vecchia, where he was working on the stupendous horse of clay, and go straight to the Grazie; climbing on the scaffolding, he would pick up a brush and give one or two brushstrokes to one of the figures, and then go elsewhere." (Kemp 1981, p.180)

It must be noted that according to Bandello, Leonardo was working simultaneously on the clay model of the *Sforza Horse* and the *Last Supper*. Since work on the 'great horse' seems to have been stopped during 1494-5, and since the "one or two brushstrokes" Bandello talks about can only refer to a very advanced stage of the work on the mural, we must suppose that Bandello was referring to a period closer to 1492-3 than 1494-5. Another confirmation of this dating is given from the technique Leonardo employed: not a *buon fresco* which demands very quick execution, but a mixed technique based on tempera and oil so that he could paint very slowly, adding each day Bandello's "one or two brushstrokes". We know that the painting was completed at the end of 1497 and we may imagine that it was necessary to Leonardo to take at least five or six years to execute it, including in this period the time needed for the preparatory studies. The well-known sheet at Windsor (**10**), a very early stage in the study of the entire composition, may therefore be dated 1492-3,[7] bearing in mind especially its relation to the scientific studies of these years. Furthermore, the beautiful head studies at Windsor (**31** and **88-89**; and Popham 1946, pl.168), which show refinement of form and elegant style, are the last of a series of which the intermediate studies - those in which Leonardo may have tested different solutions in order to represent the groups and the attitudes of the Apostles - are lost.

The particular technique Leonardo chose for the *Last Supper* is responsible, in great part at least, for its deterioration. This began soon after it had been completed, as Antonio de'Beatis, who visited the Supper in 1517-18 noted: "most excellent, although it is beginning to be spoiled, due either to the dampness of the wall or to some other accident." Other observations and records about the state of preservation of the painting include Vasari's, who said that the work "was so badly done that nothing can be seen any more but a faded smudge", and Lomazzo's, who affirms that the painting was done in oil on an unsuitable *imprimatura*. Other ancient sources speak about the humidity of the wall, and of the condensation on the surface of the painting, with water running over it on days of 'vento di tramontana'.[8]

To this already serious situation were added the interventions of the first 'restorers', Michelangelo Bellotti, who in 1726 did a number of reworkings in tempera or gouache and revarnished the entire wall in oil, and Giuseppe Mazza, who in 1770 set himself to remove Bellotti's repainting, using a scraper and filling in the gaps with an oil mixture, particularly on St Bartholomew and, to a lesser extent, on Sts James and Andrew. In a careful inspection carried out in 1802, Andrea Appiani identified the dampness of the wall as the cause of flaking of the paint surface, and recognized that it was impossible to transfer the mural painting altogether to a new support. In 1821 Stefano Barezzi made an attempt, limited to the area of the tablecloth under the figures of St Bartholomew and Christ, to see whether a transfer could in fact be made by consolidating the painting with glue and adding coloured wax-based stuccoes. Again in 1853-5, Barezzi intervened on the whole surface, consolidating and cleaning it. On the table under the figure of Christ, Barezzi's incisions which delimit the areas where he tried in vain to strip off the painting are still perfectly visible today. Because this procedure led to the collapse of a lot of original paintwork, he filled the lacunae with a wax-based material.

---

[7] The more traditional dating, around 1495-96, is that accepted in the catalogue of the recent Hayward Gallery exhibition; see entry for **10**, Catalogue 1989, p.60.

[8] For a summary of the previous campaigns of restoration and quotations from early sources, see B. Fabjan,"Il Cenacolo nuovamente restaurato", in *Leonardo. La pittura*, (ed. cit. in n.1), Florence 1985, pp.90-94; and P. Brambilla Barcilon, *Il Cenacolo di Leonardo in Santa Maria delle Grazie. Storia, condizioni, problemi*, "Quaderni di restauro" 2, Milan 1984.

Fortunately, subsequent restorers did not add other colours to Leonardo's painting, and tried only to consolidate it. In 1908 Luigi Cavenaghi engaged in a similar operation; but in 1924 Oreste Silvestri again applied plaster stuccoes around the edges of Leonardo's surviving colour, with a very disturbing result still visible today (he signed and dated his 'restoration' at the centre of the right wall, above St Matthew's shoulder). The damage resulting from the bombing of 1943 and the consequent reconstruction of the Refectory east wall was enormous. More dust and condensed humidity was produced by the rebuilding of the wall, the ceiling and the floor; so that Fernanda Wittgens, the Superintendent at that time, found the painting darkened and dimmed, and "at the least touch not only the paint but also the underlying chalk priming came away." In 1947 Mauro Pelliccioli began to fix the flakes of paint to the plaster by brushing on de-waxed shellac dissolved in alcohol and injecting casein behind it. The shellac gave the paint cohesion, consistency and a lively colour again, so it was possible to go on to the next stage. In 1951-2 and 1954, Pelliccioli worked at recovering Leonardo's original paint, especially where "the 18th-century colours had hidden the brilliant treasure of Leonardo's own painting."

I have traced a brief history of the previous restorations in order to make clear, when the decision to start a new restoration was reached at the end of the 1970s, how difficult and complicated was the situation of the original layers of Leonardo's colours, and what kind of different materials had been added to the painting during the previous four centuries. In the three decades after Pellicioli's operation, a thick layer of dust and smog had been deposited on the painting. Added to the previous substances laid onto the paint surface, this produced a new darkening and made reading Leonardo's masterpiece very difficult. Preliminary inspections with a view to a new cleaning were begun in 1976 by the Soprintendenza per i Beni Artistici e Storici di Milano. Thanks to the progress of scientific and technical knowledge, it was possible to do analyses and tests of all the chemical, physical, environmental, static, structural and climatic conditions, and as well an exhaustive and detailed photographic campaign of documentation which includes ultra-violet and infra-red photos.

At the same time, Carlo Bertelli tried to define a new methodology of restoration which aimed to recover all that remains of Leonardo's own paint, removing almost all the repaintings, and particularly those which have to a large extent concealed the original paint up to now. Overpaintings have not been removed, however, from the painted ceiling; nor from the painted tapestries, because it was clear that nothing of Leonardo's paint was concealed beneath them. In removing the 18th-century additions, especially from the heads, the hands, the draperies of the figures, and the table, a new colour sequence has appeared. With this operation, the complex and already delicate mechanical state of the pigments is also being consolidated. Problems in the actual restoration, executed by Pinin Brambilla Barcilon, include the detachment of flakes of paint and ground, and variable reactions of humidity and heat. The scientific researches set in train at the time the restoration began have demonstrated that Leonardo in fact painted on two layers of preparation, that is, in a way very similar to that used in panel painting.[9] The pigment does not always adhere to the two layers of preparation, and in turn the two layers of preparation do not always adhere to the wall. This explains why the surface appears to be very damaged, with cracks, lacunae in the colour, and flaking from the preparatory layers.

Recent analyses have also shown that the relative humidity of the wall, as well as the overpainting, affects the legibility of the colour. Thanks to the central heating and to the electric lighting, for example, the heating of the paint surface has stimulated the absorption of dust and of polluting particles, as a result of which the picture has darkened. The chromatic effect is furthermore partially altered by the adherence of dust, introduced into the Refectory on currents of air and by crowds of visitors. The dust has accumulated not only along the upper part of each flake of colour, but also along the vertical and oblique edges to the right of each flake, due to the directions of the air currents (**plate 7**). As a result, the atmospheric pollution and its accumulation in the small breaks and cracks in the pigment has created a sort of fog, a sfumato that was certainly not intended but which has strongly affected our perception of the colour, and perhaps even the design, of Leonardo's mural.[10]

The present restoration technique has made it possible to recover passages of great beauty and subtlety. The figure of St Simon on the extreme right (**plate 8**, figure at right) has regained its volume and monumentality, and its iridescent pink and white hues; the noble profile and emotion of St Matthew (**plate 9**; and **plate 8**, figure at left) have been fully revealed; the head of St James the Greater (**plate 11**, and detail on **plate 12**) has now a new plasticity and dramatic force. Even the smallest areas, when seen in their original paint, are of immensely high quality, with also a surprising quality of light which seems even to regenerate the surrounding zones where only the ground appears (**plate 10**).

However, the consequences of this restoration are not limited to the discovery of the original colour and light of Leonardo's *Last Supper*. The most important consequence is, in my opinion, the confirmation of the date

---

[9] See H. Travers Newton, "Leonardo da Vinci as Mural Painter", *Arte Lombarda* 66, 1983, pp.71-88; and the summary in the lecture on *Leonardo's Techniques*, pp.39-40 above.

[10] See my communication "Changes in the Appearance of Leonardo's Last Supper in consequence of dust and pollution" presented to the conference "The Great Age of Fresco from Masaccio to Titian. From Restoration to Interpretatio", Metropolitan Museum of Art, New York, 10-11 March 1989, now published in *Kermes. Arte e Tecnica del restauro*, no.7, Jan.-April 1990, pp.3-9.

for a long time accepted by scholars for the *Virgin, Child, St Anne and St John* cartoon now in the National Gallery in London (**fig. 28**) which has recently been dated around 1508. The simultaneous restoration of both mural and cartoon shows the same style, the same way of grouping the figures, the same solid monumentality, and, if this is possible, the same subtlety of colour (the colour of the Cartoon being suggested by the use of black chalk mixed with white, in an almost infinite variety of tones). It is impossible to consider here a number of drawings of about the same time (between the end of the 15th and the beginning of the following century), which demonstrate a period of execution for the London Cartoon soon after the execution of the *Last Supper*.[11] It is sufficient to note that if seen in mirror-image the heads of Sts Simon and Taddeus, and especially the heads of Sts James and Thomas, are almost identical in their juxtaposition to the heads of the Virgin and St Anne in the London Cartoon. In its strong contrast in this respect to the Louvre *Virgin, Child, St Anne and a Lamb* (**fig. 29**), the Leonardo Cartoon seems to be an ideal extrapolation of the scene we can see in the Refectory of Sta Maria delle Grazie in Milan, as though the two female figures had also been invited to this Supper.

Pietro C. Marani

---

[11] I have developed this point in my booklet *Leonardo. Catalogo completo dei dipinti*, Florence 1989, pp.103-4; and much further in my lecture "I dipinti di Leonardo 1500-1507: per una cronologia" held at the conference "Leonardo, Michelangelo and Raphael in Renaissance Florence, 1500-1508", Georgetown University, Villa Le Balze, Fiesole, 14 June 1989 (publication forthcoming).

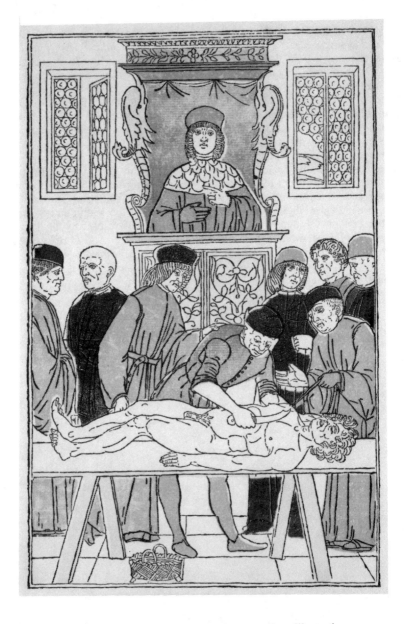

**ill.A** *An anatomical demonstration,* woodcut illustration
in Mondino dei Luzzi, *De omnibus humani corporis,*
Venice 1500.

# An introduction to Leonardo's anatomical drawings

In this lecture I will attempt to answer some simple questions connected with Leonardo's anatomical studies. The questions (in brief) are When? How? Why? and To what effect?

The first question may be answered on two levels: by placing Leonardo within the earlier anatomical tradition, and by reviewing Leonardo's anatomical work in the context of his other activities. Until well into the 16th century the authority of the writings of Galen (d. 201 AD) was absolute in anatomical teaching, so much so that in 1559, for instance, the Royal College of Physicians in London forced one of their number, Dr. Geynes, to retract his statement listing 22 inaccurate passages in Galen's work. Galen had himself undertaken no human dissection; indeed none was allowed in Imperial Rome. His 130 treatises were therefore written on the basis of his surgical experience, and from animal dissections.

The teaching of anatomy based on Galen's writings continued in Italy throughout the Middle Ages. From 1240 it was laid down that all surgeons must learn anatomy for at least one year. One human dissection was carried out at Salerno University every five years. However it was only with Mondino dei Luzzi (1276-1326) that human dissection became an essential part of the anatomical curriculum. In 1315 the body of an executed female was dissected by Mondino, for the benefit of students and members of the public alike. Mondino's treatise, *De Omnibus Humani Corporis* (first published Padua, 1487; illustrated edition Venice, 1500), was in effect a guide to dissection. But Mondino did not presume to question the authority of Galen and therefore repeated his erroneous statements concerning spherical stomachs and five-lobed livers. A few select images may suggest the type of anatomical diagram or illustration available during Leonardo's lifetime: drawings of squatting figures from Persian anatomical treatises, the woodcut illustrations to Magnus Hundt's *Anthropologium* (1501) and to Albertus Magnus, *Philosophia Pauperum*, one of the books owned by Leonardo: these could be summarized as rudimentary, over-simplified, and downright misleading. We have visible reminders of current practices in the "Blood-letting man" (from Ketham's *Fasciculus*) and in an illustration to the 1500 edition of Mondino's treatise showing an anatomical dissection under way (**ill.A**). In this woodcut the position of the Professor's chair is aloof from the corpse, and the 'Demonstrator' is there entirely to 'demonstrate' received truths, rather than to encourage research into uncharted areas of human anatomy. It is in this context that Leonardo's statement (of c.1508) should be read:

"You who say that it is better to look at an anatomical demonstration than to see these drawings would be right, if it were possible to observe all the details shown in these drawings in a single figure, in which with all your ability you will not see, nor acquire knowledge of more than a few vessels." (Windsor 19070v; Royal Academy catalogue 1977, p.20)

We know that Leonardo owned a small number of anatomical text books, including the 1500 edition of Mondino (part of Ketham's *Fasciculus*). His anatomical studies began in earnest only in the years around 1490, when Leonardo was in his late thirties. Before this time he appears to have been content to examine and draw the external anatomy of a human being or an animal, rather than probing below the surface. The list of items made before he moved from Florence to Milan in c.1482 included

"many throats of old women
many heads of old men
many complete nude figures
many arms, legs, feet and poses...
a head of an old man with a long chin"
(Kemp/Walker 1989, p.263)

Without evidence to the contrary we must assume that these were drawings, approximately of the type of Windsor 12598 (Clark/Pedretti 1968, p.121), which was however produced a few years later.

The series of anatomical drawings on blue prepared paper (Windsor 12608-12616, 12618, 12626-8; Clark/Pedretti 1968, pp.124-8 and 130-1) is normally dated to the later 1480s. In certain cases the main studies, executed in metalpoint, have faded so that they are invisible to the naked eye. However, examination under ultra-violet light renders them fully visible. The fact that Albrecht Dürer copied some of these drawings prompts one to enquire exactly when and where he had access to them. Leonardo's studies demonstrate the results of animal dissections, carried out on a dog and a monkey. There are also small-scale diagrams of human anatomy, the accuracy of which suggests unfamiliarity (if not ignorance) of the actual appearance of the dissected human form. This inaccuracy is greatest when concerned with the main organs of the body, which are shown set out in a 'situs figure', as produced by a medieval anatomist (**plate 6**). Other drawings show the musculature and skeleton of the limbs. There are also small references to the skull, the first area of the human body to be explored in depth by Leonardo. The artist's dependence on the untried theories of his contemporaries and predecessors is clear when we compare other representations of the three circular ventricles (shown, for instance, in a woodcut illustration) to those in Leonardo's drawing.

The reason behind the exquisite series of small studies of the skull made in 1489 was surely Leonardo's desire to plot the exact position of the 'senso commune', the seat of the soul, within the head (Windsor 19057-9;

1. Leonardo da Vinci, *Study of the sleeve of the Angel in the Uffizi
'Annunciation'*, Oxford, Christ Church 0036.
Pen and ink on paper; 81 x 94 mm.

2. Leonardo da Vinci, *Sequential studies of a man hammering*, detail
from Windsor, Royal Library 19149-52v **(97)**.
Pen and ink on paper; 60 x 80 mm.

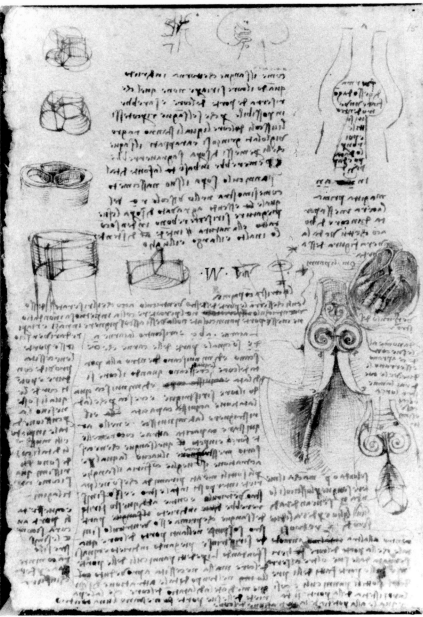

3. Leonardo da Vinci, *Blood flow within an aortic valve, and plans for a model of a valve*, Windsor, Royal Library 19082r. Pen and ink on blue paper; 283 x 207 mm.

4. Baccio Bandinelli (after Leonardo da Vinci), *Annunciate Gabriel*.
Whereabouts unknown (Christie's sale 1.7.1969 lot 119).
Pen and ink on paper; 356 x 265 mm.

5. after Leonardo da Vinci (attributed to Andrea Commodi), *Central section
of the 'Battle of Anghiari'*. Private collection (Christie's sale 25.6.1974 lot 42).
Pen and ink on paper; 142 x 267 mm.

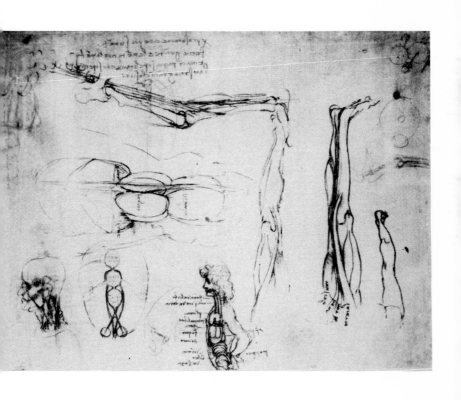

6. Leonardo da Vinci, *'Situs figure', and studies of legs.*
Windsor, Royal Library 12627r, photographed under ultraviolet light.
Pen and ink, over silverpoint, on blue prepared paper; 222 x 290 mm.

7. Leonardo da Vinci, *Last Supper*, magnified detail of surface showing deposits of dust along flakes of colour.
Milan, Refectory of Sta Maria delle Grazie.

8. Leonardo da Vinci, *Last Supper*, detail (during restoration)
of the group of Apostles at far right.
Milan, Refectory of Sta Maria delle Grazie.

9. Leonardo da Vinci, *Last Supper*, detail (during restoration)
of the head of St Matthew.
Milan, Refectory of Sta Maria delle Grazie.

10. Leonardo da Vinci, *Last Supper*, detail (during restoration)
of the table in front of St Simon.
Milan, Refectory of Sta Maria delle Grazie.

11. Leonardo da Vinci, *Last Supper*, detail (during restoration)
of the group of Apostles to right of centre.
Milan, Refectory of Sta Maria delle Grazie.

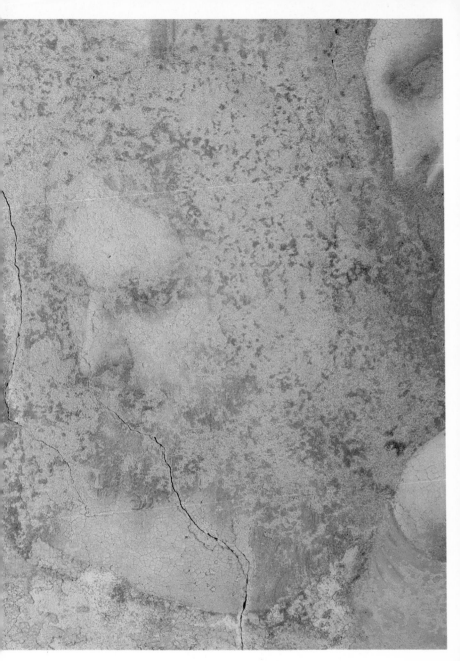

12. Leonardo da Vinci, *Last Supper*, detail (during restoration)
of the head of St James the Greater.
Milan, Refectory of Sta Maria delle Grazie.

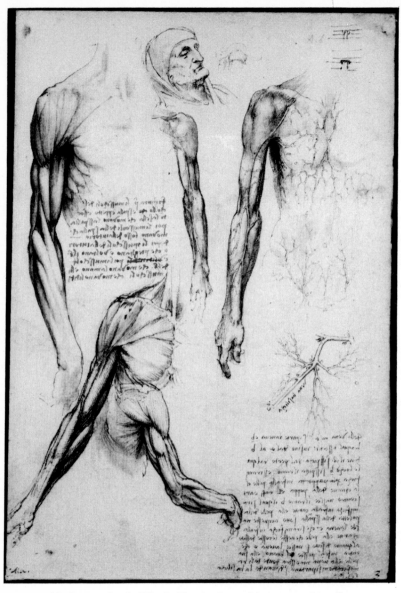

13. Leonardo da Vinci, *Head of an old man, and studies
of the muscles of the right arm.* Windsor, Royal Library 19005r.
Pen and ink on paper; 285 x 195 mm.

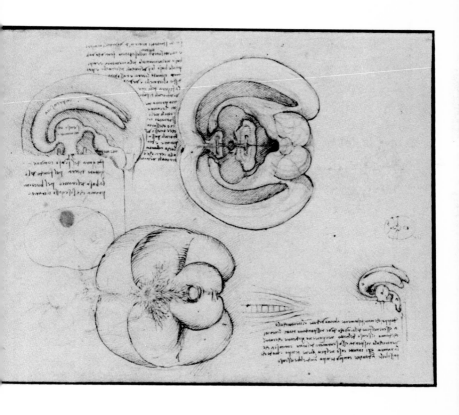

14. Leonardo da Vinci, *The brain injected to demonstrate the shapes of the cerebral ventricles*. Windsor, Royal Library 19127r.
Pen and ink, with black chalk, on paper; 200 x 262 mm.

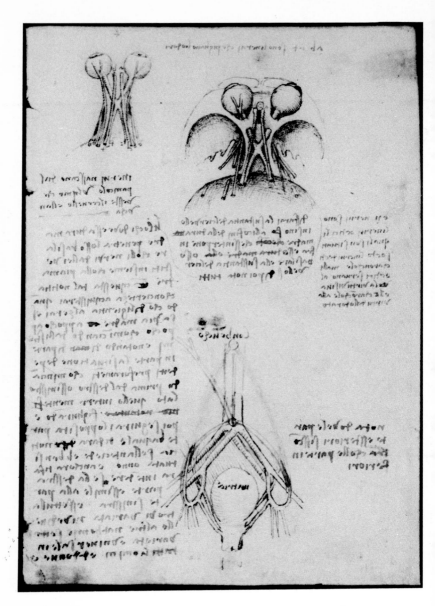

15. Leonardo da Vinci, *The optic chiasma and cranial nerves.*
Windsor, Royal Library 19052r.
Pen and ink, over black chalk, on paper; 136 x 190 mm.

16. Leonardo da Vinci, *Studies of fighting soldiers, and other sketches.*
Turin, Biblioteca Reale 15567.
Pen and ink on paper; 250 x 195 mm.

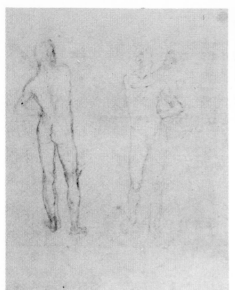

17. Leonardo da Vinci,
*Nude man seen from the front and back.*
Windsor, Royal Library 12631v.
Black chalk on paper; 190 x 139 mm.

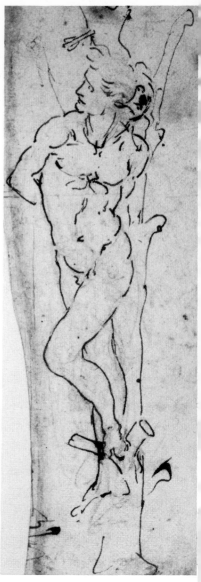

18. Leonardo da Vinci, *St Sebastian.*
Hamburg, Kunsthalle 21354.
Pen and ink on paper; 174 x 64 mm.

Clark/Pedretti 1969, p.24; see **9, 93** and **figs.38-39**). For us such a purpose accords ill with the astonishing accuracy with which the bony structure of the skull is depicted, each layer and outline indicated by the finest ink line, shadows rendered by areas of brilliantly controlled parallel vertical hatching lines.

During the 1490s, while Leonardo was continuing his work on the *Sforza Horse* and was painting the *Last Supper*, there was only limited anatomical activity. However, the study of the external appearance of the human form (and in particular of the face: see the head studies for the *Last Supper*) was intensified, as was Leonardo's search for the system of proportions underlying the relationship between the different parts of the human (and equine) form (**91**, and Windsor 12304r; Clark/Pedretti 1968, pp.17-18). That his knowledge of man's internal organs was still based almost entirely on information gleaned from earlier textbooks is proved by the 'situs figure', entitled 'tree of the veins' (**50**) which is dated to the 1490s. Leonardo's study of animal anatomy also continued in these years: a series of studies of the external anatomy of a bear (**37**, and Windsor 12372-5; Clark/Pedretti 1968, p.52) were probably drawn after an expedition in the Chiavenna mountains, near Milan, mentioned in Leonardo's notes.

Leonardo left Milan in 1499, with the collapse of Sforza rule and the French occupation of Milanese territories. During the next seven years, when he was chiefly living again in Florence, he appears to have undertaken little if any anatomical study. However from c.1506, when he returned once more to Milan - this time to work for the French - there was a renewed burst of activity. Most of Leonardo's best-known anatomical drawings should indeed be dated during the seven-year period c.1506-13. These consist of Folio B, the small format pages of c.1505-8, which share a common sheet-size with the earlier series of drawings of the skull; the larger format Folio A of c.1509-12, with the magnificent drawings of the skeleton and musculature, particularly of the arms and legs; the drawings of embryology (c.1510-12) and of the heart (c.1513); and in addition the extraordinary female anatomy (**52**) of c.1507, showing both the extent and the limitations of Leonardo's anatomical knowledge at precisely the moment that he was working on the painting of the *Mona Lisa*.

This was also the moment of Leonardo's dissection of the body of the centenarian, whose death was described on one of the pages of Folio B (Windsor 19027v; Clark/Pedretti 1969, p.13):

> "An old man a few hours before his death told me that he passed a hundred years, and that he did not feel any bodily deficiency other than weakness. And thus while sitting on a bed in the hospital of Santa Maria Nuova in Florence, without any movement or sign of distress he passed away from this life. And I made an anatomy of him in order to see the cause of so sweet

a death..." (Royal Academy catalogue 1977, pp.17-18)

The corpse shown in one of the Windsor drawings (**plate 13**) could be the subject of this passage, although it is thought to date from a year or two later, c.1509. The series to which it belongs (Folio A) includes the magnificent drawings of shoulders (e.g. **95-96**, and Windsor 19003r), feet (e.g. Windsor 19003v), ribs and legs (Windsor 19012r) and hands (e.g. Windsor 19009v; for the whole series see Clark/Pedretti 1969, pp.2-8). But Leonardo also returned to the skull, to learn the true shape of the brain by injecting an ox's brain with molten wax (**plate 4**). He examined the anatomy of the lungs (**54**), and on a single sheet of Folio B (**25**) he drew with exquisite skill a calf in utero, and - on the other side of the sheet - the 'anatomy of a smile'. This prepares us, therefore, for the final series of drawings of 'the babe in the womb', the 'great mystery' of the foetus within the waters of the mother's womb (**26**), and the studies (in pen on blue paper) of the movement of blood through the valves of the heart (**19**, and Windsor 19071; Clark/Pedretti 1969, p.30). After these drawings of c.1513, Leonardo appears to have carried out little if any anatomical work.

The artist's last years were spent first in Rome, and then in France, where a visitor, one Antonio de'Beatis, reported in 1517:

> "This gentleman has compiled a particular treatise of anatomy, with the demonstration in draft not only of the members, but also of the muscles, nerves, veins, joints, intestines and of whatever can be reasoned about in the bodies both of men and women, in a way that has never yet been done by any other person. All which we have seen with our eyes; and he said that he had already dissected more than thirty bodies both men and women of all ages." (Clark 1976, pp.157-8)

There is no question, then, that Leonardo's drawings were carried out following anatomical dissections. It is our great good fortune that the artist's extraordinary visual powers and skills as a draughtsman ensured that what he saw was recorded, and that succeeding generations have preserved most (but by no means all) of the drawings for posterity. The task that Leonardo set himself to complete, which would eventually constitute the treatise on anatomy seen by de'Beatis, was encyclopaedic.

> "This plan of mine of the human body will be unfolded to you just as though you had the natural man before you. The reason is that if you wish to know thoroughly the parts of man after he has been dissected you must either turn him, or your eye, so that you examine him from different aspects, from below, above, and from the sides... But you must understand that such knowledge

as this will not continually satisfy you on account of the very great confusion which must arise from the mixture of membranes with veins, arteries, nerves, tendons, muscles, bones and the blood which itself tinges every part with the same colour... Therefore it becomes necessary to have several dissections: you will need three in order to have a complete knowledge of the veins and arteries: three others for a knowledge of the membranes: three for the nerves, muscles and ligaments; three for the bones and cartilages, and three for anatomy of the bones, for these have to be sawn through in order to show which are hollow and which not... Three also must be devoted to the female body, and in this there is great mystery by reason of the womb and its foetus..." (Windsor 19061r; Royal Academy catalogue 1977, p.19)

Elsewhere, on a page datable c.1508 (Windsor 19070v), Leonardo himself describes some of the 'atmosphere' in which these dissections were carried out:

"...And as one single body did not suffice for sufficiently long a time it was necessary to proceed by stages with as many bodies as would render my knowledge complete: and this I repeated twice in order to discover the differences.

But though possessed of an interest in the subject you may perhaps be deterred by natural repugnance, or if this does not restrain you than perhaps by the fear of passing the night hours in the company of these corpses, quartered and flayed, and horrible to behold. And if this does not deter you then perhaps you may lack the skill in drawing essential for such representation and even if you possess this skill it may not be combined with a knowledge of perspective, while if it is so combined you may not be versed in the methods of geometrical demonstration, or the methods of estimating the forces and power of the muscles; or you may perhaps be found wanting in patience so that you will not be diligent.

Concerning which things, whether or no they have all been found in me, the hundred and twenty books which I have composed will give their verdict, yes or no. In these I have not been hindered either by avarice or negligence, but only by want of time. Farewell." (Royal Academy catalogue 1977, pp.20-1)

Lack of time, combined with almost manic attention to detail, and an irrepressibly enquiring mind, ensured that Leonardo's anatomical work was never completed, and never properly organised.

Leonardo's anatomical method appears to have developed pragmatically, as the need arose. The early studies of the skull (e.g. **93**) show the bone substance carefully (one might say 'scientifically') sectioned to reveal the detailed structure. The skeleton was naturally the easiest area to deal with, and is therefore drawn more accurately than internal organs (such as the lungs, or heart), which - in the absence of preservatives - would have lost their form and structure after a very short time. Nevertheless Leonardo devised his own techniques to overcome some at least of the difficulties. I have already mentioned that he injected an ox's brain with molten wax in order to ascertain its form (Windsor 19127r; **plate 4**). During his detailed study of the movement of blood through the valves of the heart he also suggested making a model of a valve. He noted:

> "A form of gypsum to be inflated and a thin glass within, and then break it from head and foot by a-n. But first pour the wax into the gate of a bull's heart that you may see the true form of this gate." (Windsor 19082r; Royal Academy catalogue 1977, p.124)

In order to record the results of his dissections, Leonardo devised a number of graphic or display techniques. The bone structure, for instance, was shown in 'exploded' form, to reveal how each part fitted into the other (**109**). He progressed from the early and somewhat fantastic 'sectioned' views, slicing through bones, muscles and veins (Windsor 12617r; Clark/Pedretti 1968, pp.127-8), or through the cerebral cavity (**94**), to a clearer view of the human musculature resulting from dissection. In drawings like Windsor 19003r-v (Clark/Pedretti 1969, p.3) the muscles are represented by delicately shaded cords or pulleys, thus enabling their physical properties to be suggested. Leonardo's requirement ("This plan of mine...") that each body, and each part of a body, be shown from every side, is wonderfully demonstrated in the page of drawings of the spine (**109**). The principle is further refined in an extraordinary pair of drawings (**95-96**) in which we have an idea of slow cinematographic vision as the model is turned vertically through 180° before our eyes. Leonardo used drawing as the clearest possible demonstration of the true appearance of things. On the page of drawings of the spine (**109**) he wrote:

> "Thus you will give true knowledge of their shapes, knowledge which is impossible for either ancient or modern writers. Nor would they ever have been able to give true knowledge without an immense, tedious and confused length of writing and time. But through this very short way of drawing them from different aspects one gives a full and true knowledge of them." (Royal Academy catalogue 1977, p.80)

The diagrammatic clarity of the results of arteriosclerosis in the drawing of veins, marked 'old' and 'young' (**51**), is incontrovertible. However, before moving from a discussion of How? to an examination of Why?, we should be aware that in some cases Leonardo used graphic conventions to depict what might have been rather than what actually is (or was): his drawings of the nerves and muscles of the neck and shoulders (**111**, and Windsor 19075v; Clark/Pedretti 1969, p.31) or even of the 'tree of nerves' (Windsor 19034v; Clark/Pedretti 1969, pp.15-16) are diagrammatic demonstrations, showing putative lines of direction, support and force rather than the real structure of the body. Likewise the unnervingly live heads on many of Leonardo's flayed corpses are surely not what they appear to be.

The raison d'être of Leonardo's anatomical work is many-faceted and complex. But the artist's restless curiosity must have provided the main impetus. In the two following quotes, Leonardo expressed in his own words the importance for him of proof by experience, and the need for a complete rather than an abbreviated view of the whole:

> "Many will think they may reasonably blame me by alleging that my proofs are opposed to the authority of certain men held in the highest reverence by their inexperienced judgements; not considering that my works are the issue of pure and simple experience, who is the one true mistress." (CA, f.119va; Richter 1970, I pp.116-17)

> "Abbreviators do harm to knowledge and to love, seeing that the love of anything is the offspring of this knowledge, the love being the more fervent in proportion as the knowledge is more certain... Of what use then is he who abridges the details of those matters of which he professes to give thorough information, while he leaves behind the chief part of the things of which the whole is composed? It is true that impatience, the mother of stupidity, praises brevity, as if such persons had not life long enough to serve them to acquire a complete knowledge of one single subject, such as the human body; and then they want to comprehend the mind of God in which the universe is included, weighing it minutely and mincing it into infinite parts, as if they had to dissect it!" (Windsor 19084; Richter 1970, II pp.250-1)

Leonardo's curiosity caused him to attempt to locate the soul within the head, to explain optical vision and thus to demonstrate the optic chiasma for the first time (**plate 5**), to study the changed positions of the bones in the arm in pronation and supination (**106**), to compare the skeleton of the legs of man and horse (**15**), and then to examine the 'great mystery' of the foetus in utero, whether of cow (**25**) or human (**26**). But as Martin Kemp has so vividly shown in his lecture, Leonardo's ultimate aim was to remake nature, to show the interrelatedness and the underlying laws of the natural world, and to demonstrate how man is a lesser world. These intellectual goals alone more than justified the anatomical work undertaken by Leonardo.

The possibility that Leonardo may have wished his anatomical work to be widely disseminated (or at least to be available to others) is something about which we have tantalisingly little information. The fact that Dürer saw and copied some of his early drawings indicates that those drawings, at least, were not secreted away by the artist. And the language in which Leonardo's anatomical notes are set out certainly suggests that they were intended to be read by someone other than himself. The following particularly explicit account tells of the techniques used in the latter part of the experiment involving the injection of wax into the ox's brain:

> "Ease away the brain substance from the borders of the dura mater [the hardest of the three membranes surrounding the brain]... Then note all the places where the dura mater penetrates the basilar bone with nerves unsheathed in it, together with the pia mater [the innermost of the three membranes surrounding the brain]. And you will acquire such knowledge with certainty when you diligently raise the pia mater, little by little, commencing from the edges and noting bit by bit, the situation of the aforesaid perforations, commencing first from the right or left side, and drawing this in its entirety." (Royal Academy catalogue 1977, p.48)

Antonio de'Beatis described the anatomical drawings that he saw as 'a treatise of anatomy', and several of the pages of anatomical notes and drawings that have come down to us are set out with the clarity and regularity of a printed page. Did Leonardo intend his work to be published? The following passage is practically all that we have from Leonardo's pen to help us answer this interesting question. The words appear on the lower margin of the page of studies of the spine (**109**); the final word is tantalisingly illegible:

> "And in order to give this benefit to men I teach ways of reproducing and arranging it, and I pray you, O successors, not to be parsimonious by getting them printed in..." (Catalogue 1989, p.194)

Had such a work come into print, it would surely have been very fully illustrated. For as we have already seen, Leonardo was well aware of the superiority of the image over the written word for the transmission of 'true knowledge'.

A further justification for Leonardo's anatomical drawings was also naturally

60

to be found in his other artistic activities. In his own words,

> "It is a necessary thing for the painter, in order to be good at arranging parts of the body in attitudes and gestures which can be represented in the nude, to know the anatomy of the sinews, bones, muscles and tendons. He should know their various movements and force, and which sinew or muscle occasions each movement, and paint only those distinct and thick, and not the others, as do many who, in order to appear to be great draughtsmen, make their nudes wooden and without grace, so that they seem a sack full of nuts rather than the surface of a human being, or indeed, a bundle of radishes rather than muscular nudes." (McMahon 1956, p.129)

This passage inevitably leads on to our final question: "To what effect?" Leonardo's artistic development can be seen on various levels, and the *Last Supper* as the key work in which his chief advances may be seen. For our purposes, the great range of facial expression and of gesture in the mural painting are the crucial elements, far surpassing what any earlier artist had ever been able to suggest. It is ironic that the *Last Supper* shows Leonardo painting with anatomical competence areas of the body - particularly the face and hands - which he does not appear to have examined in detail until around a decade later: this makes one wonder, have we lost *so* many drawings? Likewise the *Battle of Anghiari* was to show men and horses in action in a variety of positions and activities, with a verisimilitude that had never been encountered before and which would surely have been impossible without the benefit of the artist's anatomical explorations. In Leonardo's few later paintings the human figure is never shown in action and although the artist's firm knowledge of anatomical structure is constantly apparent, a painting such as the *St John the Baptist* (fig.33) reveals how the muscles and skeleton eventually become totally imperceptible below the smoothly modelled flesh. In drawings the progression from the tentatively modelled metalpoint nude (Windsor 12637; Clark/Pedretti 1968, pp.123-4) to the magnificent back view in red chalk (32) cannot be completed by a third, late, example, for (significantly) there are no late drawings of nudes.

The usefulness of the anatomical drawings for other branches of Leonardo's activity is plain if we look at the flying machine alone: the great structure - intellectual as well as mechanical - which symbolized the recent exhibition at the Hayward Gallery. Without first examining how human beings move, and how birds fly (e.g. 107), and by taking notes and drawings during these examinations, Leonardo would surely never have embarked on this ambitious project.

This discussion must end by mentioning the effect of Leonardo's anatomical work on the history of anatomical knowledge. The answer is sadly negative because until the start of the present century the results of his research were unavailable to the medical world. His "discoveries" therefore had to be repeated by others, in the mainstream of scientific research. Now that we can look back and see how much he knew (or almost knew), centuries in advance of others, his achievements and their tragic futility are all the more apparent.

Jane Roberts

# The moving figure in Leonardo's art

The title of this lecture requires a few words of explanation for, on the surface at least, it goes somewhat against the grain of the recent Leonardo exhibition. As I see it, one of the aims of the exhibition was to break down the distinction between Leonardo the artist and Leonardo the scientist for, as Professor Gombrich pointed out in his prefatory essay to the exhibition catalogue, it is a distinction which Leonardo himself would probably not have recognised (Catalogue 1989, pp.1-4). Leonardo, suggests Gombrich, would not have made a distinction between his 'scientific' drawings, whether they be drawings of human and plant anatomy, natural forces or war machines, and those which he made in preparation for his paintings. To him, they would have been part of the same activity, part of his quest for a universal science based on the empirical study of nature.

The arrangement of the drawings within the exhibition maintained this view, with its fascinating combination and juxtaposition of studies for paintings with more straightforward studies of the natural world. Why then, have I placed the emphasis on the moving figure in Leonardo's art? Why not the moving figure in Leonardo's work - or even in Leonardo's universal science? The point I wish to make is that the specifically artistic context of Leonardo's activity did in fact impinge on his work on many occasions, and in quite significant ways. While Leonardo's empirical, scientific vision affected the nature of his art, his career as an artist also affected his approach to the natural world, and nowhere more so than in his approach to the moving figure.

The nature and significance of Leonardo's studies of the moving figure cannot be wholly explained in terms of a direct, spontaneous rendering of nature, one which he then transferred into his works in painting. His drawings and paintings of the moving figure should not be seen simply either as one facet of a self-contained universal science, or as part of a unified personal project with no relation to the community of artists and viewers around him. In large measure, Leonardo's studies of the moving figure were both circumscribed and conditioned by the conventions of art in his time, as well as by the social and cultural milieu of which he was a part.

This point is particularly important in view of the fact that both the exhibition and the catalogue throw into sharp relief the empirical basis of Leonardo's work, and his insistence on the primacy of visual experience. In front of the works themselves, it is difficult not to be struck by the apparent spontaneity and directness of Leonardo's response to and depiction of the natural world, especially in a work such as the *Last Supper* (**fig.25**), and in its compositional study (**10**). If we compare the *Last Supper* with the version by Andrea del Castagno, painted for Sant'Apollonia in Florence probably between 1447 and 1449, we are inevitably struck by the immediacy and naturalness of the disciples' agitated movement in Leonardo's version - their violent reactions to Christ's actions and pronouncement. There is, in short, a startling realism about Leonardo's work, which leads us to think of him as someone who captured real appearances in an accurate, almost photographic way. I would suggest, however, that this is both misleading and an over-simplification, for however natural and spontaneous Leonardo's works may look they are in many ways highly artificial. Even in the *Last Supper*, the movements of the apostles are in many cases conventional. They are part of the traditional vocabulary of gesture in religious painting, albeit rendered in a more convincing and dramatic way, underlined by a surer knowledge of anatomy.[1]

As another example we could consider the Cologne sheet of figure studies for the *Adoration of the Magi* (**fig.16**), also included in the exhibition (7). At first glance the movements and attitudes of the figures appear highly natural, and may well have been taken from the life. Yet they are not simply literal transcriptions of natural movements, for three of the models have been arranged in poses familiar from antique sculpture. In other words, this is natural movement or posture seen through the lens of classical antiquity, reinterpreted, that is, in terms of contemporary artistic interests and trends.

In his studies of movement, then, Leonardo was not a simple naturalist, and his studies of the moving figure cannot be explained with reference to nature alone. Like any artist of his time, although certainly less than many, Leonardo was subject to a complex set of conventions, both artistic and cultural in the broader sense. He simply was not free to represent movement in a literal, photographic way, even assuming that he could ever have acquired the technical skill to do so. The task of this lecture is thus to illustrate the ways in which the moving figure in Leonardo's art reflects not just his scientific, empirical vision, but also the influence of artistic tradition and social codes or rules. To do so is in no way to undermine Leonardo's originality. Rather, it is to place him more clearly within the context of his time and to see him not as an isolated genius with a wholly personal and idiosyncratic vision, based on the observation of nature, but as an artist who both accepted and transformed the artistic conventions of his age.

Before going on to some individual cases, I should perhaps clarify that by artistic convention I do not mean a set of written or explicit rules which the artist had to follow, but rather a set of implicit but undeniable expectations and assumptions about the role and nature of art. Amongst these, the following are the most important for my point. Firstly, that movement in painting, whilst having a certain realism and expressing the emotions, should also be attractive to the eye - two demands which were by no means always compatible. Secondly, that movement, again whilst being expressive, should

---

[1]  For a discussion of the conventions of gesture in religious painting, see M. Baxandall, *Painting and Experience in Fifteenth-century Italy*, Oxford 1974, pp.45-71.

conform to the requirements of decorum and of propriety. Lastly, there was the expectation that religious works of art should perform certain functions, either devotional or instructive, within which movement played a crucial part.

I would now like to illustrate these points by looking at some examples of the way in which Leonardo rendered the moving figure, considering the way in which natural appearances and observation are filtered, so to speak, through the lens of art. We will start by looking at a type of form or figure which is in many ways paradigmatic of Leonardo's approach to movement - the serpentine or spiral form, which is, in fact, a particular hall-mark of his work. This spiral form, often known as the *figura serpentinata*, appears in various forms in the majority of Leonardo's surviving works, from the **Portrait of Cecilia Gallerani (fig.26)**, painted c.1485, where Leonardo uses it to bring a new animation and mobility to the conventional half-length portrait, to the drawings **(14, 75)** for the **Leda and the Swan (fig.31)**, where it reaches its most complex and abstract form. As Martin Kemp has pointed out (Catalogue 1989, p.148; and Kemp 1981, pp.270-7), the serpentine form runs through every aspect of both painting and drawing **(75)**, from the swirling pattern of Leda's hair, to the spiralling plants from which her babies wriggle into life, to the form of the swan, and lastly to that of Leda herself. This is particularly evident in the drawing, for which there are a number of subsidiary studies, such as the study of a Star of Bethlehem and other plants **(57)**.

The repetition of this form throughout the work is partly, as Kemp has suggested, Leonardo's way of expressing in abstract form his vision of the underlying unity of the world, the organic unity between human, plant and animal life, all animated by the same swirling motion. This persistent use of the spiral also gives the impression of natural and lively movement. The spiral form is, however, a highly artificial one: even the hair of Leda, for which Leonardo made preliminary studies **(58)**, was modelled from a wig. It is, as Kemp has pointed out, an abstraction and intensification of the natural propensities of hair.[2] The extension of the serpentine form to the movement of the human figure is even more of an abstraction and this is particularly apparent in the standing version **(fig.31)**. To be sure, this standing, spiral pose has its roots, at least in part, in classical contrapposto. This well-known classical pose had long been recognised as a means of suggesting potential motion in a standing figure, by articulating the uneven distribution of weight which is a precondition of movement of any kind. The figure which stands solidly on both feet has no capacity for motion: it is only when weight is unevenly distributed that movement becomes possible. The spiral form is essentially a development of this formula into three dimensions, so to speak, but which takes the form to a degree of artificiality and elegance which bears

---

[2] That Leda's hair is modelled on a wig was first pointed out by Kenneth Clark in his monograph on Leonardo (Clark 1976, p.116 n.1).

only a token resemblance to the movements of real life. It becomes, in fact, a symbol or metaphor for movement or potential movement, rather than a transcription of an actual moving figure, based on accurate observation. It is a means of suggesting continuous and highly graceful movement within a stable form.

Leonardo here conforms to the artistic demand for movement to be graceful and pleasing to the eye - a requirement which had been articulated frequently in writings on art since the beginning of the century. Not only, however, is this movement an abstraction - a compromise between nature and art, between realism and grace. It is also based, although not directly, on antique sculpture - in the case of the kneeling version on a kneeling Venus, and in that of the standing version on a Roman figure of Cupid with a Bow, after the classical Greek sculptor Lysippus. The idea that a bending and twisting form would give a figure both liveliness and grace had also been spelled out in classical texts. Although he was discussing styles of rhetoric, Quintilian used the example of sculpture to make the point that departure from the straight line, in other words, a twist of the body, creates liveliness and grace, just as departure from normal usage in speech gives interest and variety.[3]

There were, then, several well-known precedents both visual and textual for the use of this form, which recognised it as both pleasing to the eye and uniquely suggestive of motion, although itself only natural or realistic in a very broad sense. Furthermore, as has often been pointed out, Leonardo had seen it used to good effect in the workshop of his Florentine teacher Verrocchio, most successfully in his *Putto with a Dolphin* (Pope-Hennessy 1971, pl.78) executed in the 1470s, and originally intended as the centrepiece of a fountain. That is not to say, however, that Leonardo did not use the serpentine form in an innovative way. On the contrary the interest here, as with all Leonardo's moving figures, lies in the way in which he both retains, but also transforms, traditional artistic types. What is significant about the **Leda**, particularly in the standing version, is how Leonardo uses the form to explore another aspect of his interest in movement - the expression of emotion and states of mind.

In his Notebooks on art Leonardo emphasised repeatedly that movements of the body should reflect those of the mind. Thus, he writes:

> "The good painter has to paint two principal things, that is to say, man and the intention of his mind. The first is easy and the second difficult, because the latter has to be represented through gestures and movements of the limbs... The motions and postures of figures should display the true mental state of the originator of these motions, in such a way that they could not signify

---

[3] Quintilian, *Institutio oratoria* VIII, iii, 49 and 61.

anything else." (Kemp/Walker 1989, pp.144-6)

Here too, of course, Leonardo was echoing a sentiment that had already been expressed by Leon Battista Alberti in his book *On Painting* written in 1435. There is little doubt, however, that Leonardo felt the importance of this idea with particular urgency, given his intimate knowledge of the body's physiological plumbing, and his acute observation of the impact of emotions on our bodily movements.

The fascination of the *Leda* thus lies in the fact that Leonardo has deployed the graceful, mobile, serpentine form not in a wholly abstract way, but in a way which helps to express Leda's dual interests or states of mind. In the standing version, the twist of her upper body and the thrust of the hip to the right indicate her fusion with her feathery lover, while the opposite twist of her head and legs and the lowering of her eyes convey her attention to her hatching babies, who look up at her as they wriggle out of their shells. The serpentine form as pure movement is infused with the hint of Leda's states of mind, of the continuous, dual pull between lover and children. The abstract spiral thus becomes a subtly expressive instrument, conveying the two sides of Leonardo's interest - the pure, continuous movement that is characteristic of all life forms and which also gives them their special grace, and the movement which reflects our innermost thoughts, intentions and desires. It is, we could say, the perfect matching of nature and art, expression and grace, abstraction and meaning.

This dual aspect of Leonardo's achievement did not go unnoticed in the 16th century. Vasari explicitly praised Leonardo for his mastery of all aspects of nature and especially that of movement. He also praised his work for its grace - a quality which, for Vasari, was linked primarily to the movement of the human figure. Thus, Vasari wrote of Leonardo:

"...he was so favoured by nature that to whatever he turned his mind or thoughts the results were always inspired and perfect; and his lively and delightful works were incomparably graceful and realistic." (Vasari/Bull 1971, p.257)

In the Preface to Part Three of the *Lives* Vasari wrote:

"It was Leonardo who originated the third style or period, which we like to call the modern age; for in addition to the force and robustness of his draughtsmanship and his subtle and exact reproduction of every detail in nature, he showed in his works an understanding of rule, a better knowledge of order, correct proportion, perfect design, and an inspired grace." (Vasari/Bull 1971, p.252)

Vasari's appreciation of these two aspects of Leonardo's work - of what we might call nature on the one hand and art or artifice on the other - is also implicit in the position which Vasari gives Leonardo in the structure of the *Lives* as a whole.

Vasari divided the *Lives* into three parts or ages, each representing a certain stage in the development of the arts towards their final peak of perfection which he saw as having been reached in his own age, especially in the works of Michelangelo. For Vasari, this development was defined largely in terms of the conquest of real appearances, of the artist's growing ability to depict the natural world, particularly the human figure in motion. During the first two ages artists had made significant strides in the mastery of appearances, but had not brought it to its final degree of perfection. This achievement had been the province of the third age which, significantly, began with Leonardo. Thus, on the one hand, Leonardo was seen by Vasari as having brought to its final perfection the struggle for the mastery of nature which had long been the aim of art. He was seen as the culmination of a development which had been unfolding since the time of Cimabue - and in this sense, as I have suggested, he was the heir of tradition. On the other hand, Vasari also saw Leonardo as inaugurating a new era in which the mere technical mastery of movement and expression was refined by the addition of grace. It was this development which marked the final perfection of art, and it is a development of which Leonardo marked the beginning. Leonardo, in other words, stood at the threshold between tradition and innovation, nature and art.

Vasari's recognition of Leonardo's achievement was, however, even more specific than this, for it is clear from the *Lives* as a whole that Vasari's notion of grace in movement depended largely on the use of the twisting or serpentine form. Vasari also suggested that the artists of the third age learnt this technique by looking at antique sculpture, particularly works such as the *Laocöon*. In the Preface to the Part Three of the *Lives*, which directly precedes the Life of Leonardo, Vasari wrote:

> "Success came to the artists who followed (the second age) after they had seen some of the finest works of art mentioned by Pliny dug out of the earth: namely, the *Laocöon*, the *Hercules*, the great torso of Belvedere... and countless others, all possessing the appeal and vigour of living flesh and derived from the finest features of living models. Their attitudes were entirely natural and free, exquisitely graceful and full of movement." (Vasari/Bull 1971, p.251)

Implicitly, then, from the dual lesson of nature and antique sculpture, Leonardo brought to perfection the use of the serpentine form, bringing together the twin aims of realism and grace.

The nature of Leonardo's achievement can be further clarified by comparing his use of the serpentine form with Donatello's - a comparison which Vasari himself implicitly set up. Whilst chronologically Donatello belonged to the second age, the period of art which did not achieve total perfection, Vasari considered him almost worthy of being placed in the third, inaugurated by Leonardo. More important, Vasari praised Donatello for exactly those qualities which he praised in Leonardo - natural movement and grace. The two artists achieved the same ends, only with slightly different degrees of perfection corresponding to their respective positions within the overall progress of art. We can illustrate this by comparing Leonardo's standing *Leda* with the Virgin in Donatello's *Cavalcanti Annunciation* (Janson 1963, pl.43) carved between 1428 and 1433. For the figure of the Virgin Donatello used a version of the serpentine or spiral form flattened in order to accommodate the figure within the narrow space of the niche. The movement also has the same rationale as that of Leonardo's *Leda*, combining in one form two different and opposing impulses. Like Leonardo, Donatello has used the form to convey two different and conflicting emotions - the Virgin's alarm at the angel's appearance, which causes her to rise from her seat and move away to the right, and her simultaneous acknowledgement and acceptance of his message.

Vasari himself recognised this, while also emphasising the movement's exquisite grace. In his biography of Donatello he wrote:

> "Donatello's ingenuity and skill are especially apparent in the figure of the Virgin herself: frightened by the unexpected appearance of the angel she makes a modest reverence with a charming, timid movement, turning with exquisite grace towards him as he makes his salutation." (Vasari/Bull 1971, pp.174-5)

Both Donatello and Leonardo thus use the serpentine form both to express emotion through movement and to achieve grace. The difference between them is simply one of the degree of realisation: Leonardo, we could say, turned Donatello's solution from two dimensions into three, thus exemplifying the difference between the second and third ages. The serpentine form in Leonardo's art, then, is not a literal transcription of a natural movement based on empirical observation, nor is it simply another facet of Leonardo's universal science. Rather, it is both the product and the site of a complex combination of forces and ideas: a long-standing and traditional interest in naturalism in the arts, the desire for pictorial elegance and grace, the influence of antique sculpture and even of literary texts, the influence of his teacher Verrocchio and perhaps also of Donatello himself - all of which were perceived in his art by writers such as Vasari.

We should now consider the problem of movement in figure-groups for, even more than in a work such as the *Leda*, Leonardo was here constrained by artistic conventions. We can see this perhaps most clearly in Leonardo's studies for the theme of Madonna and Child, for example in the National

Gallery's cartoon of the *Virgin, Child, St Anne and St John* (**fig.28**) datable c.1505-7. This, in fact, provides a further illustration of the degree of artificiality and abstraction inherent in Leonardo's rendering of movement, for the interrelated movement of the figures is a quite improbable combination of serpentine forms. The Virgin and St Anne take up the spiral form again in overlapping layers, overlaid by the Christ child depicted in a complex and elegant fish-like movement. These complex, lively and interlocking movements have been compressed into a tight pyramidal form more clearly illustrated by the associated study (**77**) in which a dense network of energetic, overdrawn movements is compressed into a perfect pyramid.

To some extent, this packing of forms into a tight pyramidal shape may have been designed to allow Leonardo to explore another of his artistic interests - the illusion of relief which, as he said himself, was the soul and highest aim of painting. The overlapping of solid forms within a small compact area clearly emphasises the plasticity of the whole. It may also have been designed to express metaphorically the emotional or psychological unity of the religious group. More important for our purposes, however, is the possibility that Leonardo was here accommodating himself to the demands of artistic convention - this time the demands and function of religious paintings. The same tendencies can be observed in the Louvre *Virgin, Child, St Anne and a Lamb* (**fig.29**), or indeed, in almost any of his works on this theme, although not always so pronounced. While it may be true that the patrons for whom these works were destined may have seen their religious function as secondary to their being a work by Leonardo, it is nonetheless inevitable that Leonardo would have kept at least half-consciously in mind that such works were traditionally designed as devotional images. They had to fulfil certain requirements which though usually unspoken were nonetheless important. Most important amongst these was that they had to present the spectator with a calm and stable structure in order to facilitate contemplation. They also needed to provide a clear central point on which the viewer could focus. Movement which was either too vigorous, or too widely dispersed through the picture would interfere with the work's purpose as a focus for meditation, even if it might be more realistic in a strict sense.

The pyramidal form which Leonardo used is both stable and hierarchical, making the centre of attention clear, whilst providing a form of visual equilibrium. By compressing the complex, interlocking movements within this compact and stable shape, Leonardo observed the traditional function of devotional art by making the image easy to look at, at the same time giving it maximum internal mobility. Similar observations could be made with reference to Leonardo's *Adoration of the Magi* (**fig.16**). The Adoration was a subject which potentially allowed Leonardo to explore to the full his interest in vigorous and expressive movement. Here again, however, the constraints of convention are apparent in the way in which Leonardo compressed and confined the movements of his figures into interlocking geometric shapes, a pyramid within a half-circle. As an altarpiece, this painting's function was devotional and didactic and Leonardo had to compose it accordingly. The Virgin and Child, who had to be the focus of attention and devotion, are made the still apex of a pyramid, around which the vigorous movement of the crowd revolves. Even here, however, despite the innovative way in which Leonardo has presented the movements of the retinue, with their gestures of humility, amazement and awe, the actual movements of the foreground group are relatively restrained. Moreover their movement is effectively contained and brought into a visual equilibrium by the still, standing figures to the extreme left and right. The most vigorous and energetic movements are reserved for the mysterious fighting horsemen in the distance, who charge and struggle far removed from the centre of the devotional action.

Leonardo was of course not only observing the functional requirements of the piece. He was also drawing on prevailing artistic conventions, for this mode of composing altarpieces had long been employed by Florentine artists, for example by Botticelli, whose Uffizi *Adoration of the Magi* is similarly brought into equilibrium by the use of a pyramid, with the Virgin at the centre. Leonardo produced a variation on a theme - refining it firstly by bringing the figures closer together and making the grouping denser and more compact, and secondly by bringing a greater degree of animation into the crowd itself. As in the National Gallery cartoon, we could say that he turns a restriction to his advantage in that the confining geometric forms serve to accentuate the animation and confusion within. Leonardo was however not free to experiment with lively, energetic and realistic movements in any kind of formation. The need for visual clarity, equilibrium and ease of viewing was in many ways inimical to a purely natural depiction of the confusion and excitement intrinsic to the event. Thus, not only are the movements of the figures brought into a stable and coherent form, they are also relatively subdued, the most obvious movements being the gestures of the hands. Indeed it is these, rather than movements of the body as a whole, that create the overriding appearance of animation.

There is, I suggest, a further explanation for this, one which brings us to another aspect of the influence of convention on Leonardo's work. The convention in this case is not so much an artistic one as a social and cultural one which dictated the way in which eligible people should move. Leonardo had to concern himself not only with how people did move under certain conditions, that is with their natural actions and reactions, but also with how they ought to move according to social convention, particularly if they wanted to show themselves to be socially, morally and intellectually refined. Generally speaking, the educated 15th- and 16th-century audience had a sensitive perception of movement, and a more developed sense of its significance than is the case today. This sensitivity to movement sprang from two closely related roots, both of which were familiar to Leonardo. Firstly, the Renaissance viewer inherited from antiquity, and primarily from Aristotle, a system of physiology which considered that our every emotion and passion was reflected in bodily movement. According to Aristotle, this movement was brought about by a physical substance called *pneuma*, a kind of hot breath which rushed into the limbs from the heart, under the impetus of the sensitive soul. Each passing emotion propelled the *pneuma* around the body, forcing us into movement.

At the same time, Aristotle considered movement to be an index of moral character - more specifically, of what we might call moral fibre. During the Middle Ages and the Renaissance morality was defined largely in terms of restraint, and more specifically in terms of our ability to withstand the onslaught of the passions. In the moral man the passions and their effects should be restrained by the bridle of reason, and this, in turn, would be manifest in movement. A moderate movement, especially under conditions or circumstances of great emotional strain, such as the death of a daughter or the loss of a war, would be seen as a sign of moral fibre, whereas the man who flung himself to the ground in anguish would be perceived as irrational and weak. These moral and ethical qualities of moderation and reason were also a sign of education, and thus of social standing. For Aristotle, moral qualities were not inherent, but could be learnt and cultivated by experience and education. Thus a moderate movement betokened a morally educated and socially civilised man. Excess, on the other hand, was the province of the buffoon.

During the Renaissance the implications of this system of thinking about movement were emphasised by a renewed interest in other kinds of classical literature, particularly the ethical writings of men such as Cicero, who also emphasised that it was important for a man to move moderately if he was to present himself as moral and civilised. He suggested also that an understanding of the significance of movement was important in enabling us to assess the character of others within the social and political arena. From the dual root of Aristotle's physiology and Cicero's ethical writings the educated Renaissance viewer acquired an acute awareness of the moral and social significance of movement. This is reflected particularly clearly in the treatise *On Civic Life* (1439) by the Florentine humanist Matteo Palmieri who wrote to the good citizen:

"We must now talk about bodily movement and posture and what is required therein... every movement and every attitude of the body which departs from natural usage and is ugly to look at must be avoided... It is often the case that by the smallest outward signs the greatest vices are revealed, and the true nature of our soul is made manifest, as for example, a lofty glance signifies arrogance, a lowered one humility... the hands must be deployed in the appropriate way with no strange movements... being neither awkward and rigid, nor limp and dangling... In walking we must remember our age and station; do not walk rigidly, nor so slowly and ponderously that you appear pompous... Nor should you walk too fast since this is a sign of thoughtlessness and lack of constancy..."[4]

There is no doubt that the educated Renaissance public extended this sensitivity to movement in life to their perception and interpretation of movement in art. On one level this posed a problem for painters who were becoming increasingly concerned with the expressive aspect of movement and with the challenge of rendering through physical movement the surge, ebb and flow of the passions. These expressive movements were not only the painter's main narrative resource - his means of explaining the story of a painting - but also a prime demonstration of his skill, as Leonardo emphasised in his Notebooks. Furthermore, as he also pointed out, the greatest emotion should be manifested and accompanied by the greatest physical movement. On the other hand, the painter still had to remain within the bounds of the morally and socially acceptable, bounds dictated by cultural conventions such as those outlined by Palmieri. How could the painter, through one and the same movement, both give a clear and moving demonstration of emotion, and exercise the restraint which was necessary to suggest that his figures had the requisite moral and social dignity?

However great his interest in the expressive aspect of movement, Leonardo himself was very much aware of these social constraints. In his Notebooks he frequently warned the painter to avoid excess in movement, and he did so in terms which clearly recall those of Aristotle:

"Again I remind you that movements should not be so extravagant nor so excessively active that a peaceful scene seems to be a battle or a morris-dance of drunken men." (McMahon 1956, I p.155)

In a famous passage from his Notebooks, he also cited an example of a painting where he felt that the artist had taken movement beyond the bounds of dignity and appropriateness. Leonardo wrote:

"I saw, some days since, the picture of an angel who, while he was making The Annunciation, appeared to be chasing Our Lady out of her room, with movements which displayed such offensiveness as one might show to a most vile enemy, and Our Lady seemed as if she, in despair, would throw herself from a window. Bear it in mind, do not fall into any such defects."

---

[4]  M. Palmieri, *Vita civile*, ed. G. Belloni, Florence 1982, pp.95-6 (my translation).

(McMahon 1956, I p.58)

Leonardo does not identify the guilty party here, but his remark has been convincingly associated with Botticelli's Uffizi *Annunciation* in which the Virgin throws herself sideways in an exaggerated version of Donatello's *Cavalcanti Annunciation* Madonna.[5] A painting like this must have posed two problems for Leonardo. The Virgin's movement is undoubtedly expressive, but the emotion which it conveys is hardly appropriate to the event, if only because the Virgin was thought to have been used to seeing angels, having been visited by them since her earlier years. Moreover it also suggests in her a degree of moral imbalance, as well as a lack of social refinement. Her movement, in Leonardo's terms, resembles the excesses of a drunkard or a morris-dancer - of the person who has no self-control. Indeed, the movement of Botticelli's Virgin can be profitably compared with late 15th-century Florentine engravings of morris-dancers, whose leaping and bending movements are often strikingly similar.[6]

Another case, of which Leonardo seems to have been aware, of an artist being criticised for taking movement to excess again concerns Donatello. In his *Treatise on Architecture* Antonio Filarete criticised Donatello's figures of apostles on the bronze doors for the Old Sacristy in S. Lorenzo in Florence (Janson 1963, pls. 62-5).[7] He claimed that the movement of these figures was excessive and inappropriate to their station, since it made them look like fencers. The implication here is clear; apostles should look like philosophers and should show a dignity suggestive of moral and social gravity. Few Renaissance observers would have thanked you for pointing out that most of the apostles had been fishermen. They were thought of as philosophers and should thus be accorded the dignity associated with that type. Filarete's criticism failed, of course, to take into account the problem which faced Donatello in this commission, that of showing pairs of non-narrative figures in a very small format, in a way which commanded attention visually and projected a certain liveliness. There may also have been an element of sour grapes in Filarete's response here, for he himself executed two figures of apostles on his own bronze doors for St Peter's in Rome. He showed his apostles rather in the fashion of figures in Early Christian mosaics, giving them a conventional dignity and remoteness. In retrospect, however, he may well have realised that Donatello's solution, whilst unusual, was considerably

---

[5] This connection was first suggested by Baxandall, op. cit. in n.1, pp.55-6.

[6] See for example A.M. Hind, *Early Italian Engraving*, New York and London 1938, no. A.II.12 (part I, I p.68 and II plate 97).

[7] Antonio Filarete, *Treatise on Architecture*, ed. J. Spencer, New Haven and London 1965, p.306. For discussion, see Janson 1963, pp.112 and 136-7.

more interesting than his own.

Leonardo appears to have been aware of this debate. Although, characteristically, he does not mention any names, there is a passage in his Notebooks which could almost have been conceived as a reply to Filarete, whose text he certainly knew. Leonardo is discussing the problem of artists who excel in only one aspect of their art and who are thus unable to appreciate the skills of others. Some painters, he writes, dwell too much on the facial expressions of their figures and denigrate the bodily movements depicted by others. Thus:

> "their own paintings being without movement, because they themselves are languid and of little motion, they criticize that which has greater and more ready movements than are represented by them, saying that they appear possessed and like morris-dancers." (McMahon 1956, I p.58)

These conventions of movement must also have had a bearing on Leonardo's own approach to the moving figure, especially in his religious works. Within a subject like the Adoration of the Magi, it was inconceivable that the Magi could be shown in movements which were too vigorous and expressive, if they were to retain the requisite dignity. Thus, although the overall impression in Leonardo's *Adoration* is of great agitation and movement, on close observation it is clear that the majority of the movement comes from gestures of the hands, rather than from impulses of the body as a whole. Moreover the composition is closed off on either side by standing figures which epitomise the type of gravity and stillness conventionally associated with philosophers and thinkers, figures which stand in silent and dignified contemplation. These are not studies from nature, but rather Leonardo's version of a particular cultural ideal, the type of the classical philosopher. The movements in the *Adoration*, then, are not examples of straightforward naturalism, but of natural movement seen through the twin prisms of classical statuary and cultural conventions.

Perhaps the only work in which Leonardo felt able to explore fully his interest in expressive movement was the *Battle of Anghiari*, part of which is known in a copy by Rubens (**fig.32**), and through Leonardo's preliminary sketches (**13**; and Popham 1946, pl.191-201). The subject of the battle was dear to Leonardo's heart and he wrote a long description of the way in which to represent such a subject, detailing the kinds of movement which would occur in such a case (Kemp/Walker 1989, pp.228-33). He also stated quite clearly in his Notebooks that violent movements should be avoided in painting except in the case of battles (McMahon 1956, I p.110). Here, movement can go beyond the bounds of social convention as men are moved by a fury of anger and hostility. Even in Rubens' copy, we get some sense that Leonardo's interests in expression were given full rein in a work in which neither beauty, grace nor restraint were to be expected.

As a final case of Leonardo's sensitivity to social codes of movement, we can consider his drawing of a *Pointing Lady in a Landscape* (**79**) dating from around 1515. Leonardo clearly showed his awareness of contemporary social conventions when, discussing the way in which women should move, he wrote:

> "Women should be represented with modest gestures, the legs close together, the arms gathered together, heads bent and inclined to one side... Women and girls should not have their legs raised nor too far apart, because that shows boldness and general lack of modesty, while straight legs indicate timidity and modesty."
> (McMahon 1956, I pp.106 and 148; cf.Kemp/Walker 1989, p.152)

Leonardo is talking here not so much about natural movement as about how refined people should ideally behave. One example of an artist observing these conventions very closely can be seen in Domenico Ghirlandaio's fresco of the *Birth of St John the Baptist* dating from the late 1480s in the church of Sta Maria Novella in Florence. Here the visiting gentlewomen, who are of course the donors, are shown, not surprisingly, in attitudes which exemplify the notion of the virtuous woman, their feet close together so that their steps are barely perceptible, their drapery hanging accordingly in neat, orderly folds, and their arms gathered into the waist. Their movement is deliberately contrasted, in a touch of overt flattery, with that of the servant girl, with her wide stride, open legs and revealing drapery.

Leonardo's *Pointing Lady* observes many of the same conventions - her stance erect, her steps small with the knees and ankles close together, and one arm held neatly into her waist. These features could be explained by the fact that she may have been intended to illustrate a figure from Dante's *Divine Comedy*. In Canto XXVIII of the Purgatorio Dante describes the figure of Matelda, who acts as his guide until the appearance of Beatrice, and who appears to him on the banks of the River Lethe:

> "As a dancing lady turns with her feet close together
> Foot by foot set close and to the ground
> And scarcely putting one before the other
> So she to me... turned round...
> So when she'd come to where the crystalline
> Clear water bathes the grasses, she at once
> Did the grace to lift her eyes to mine...
> So upright on the other bank she smiled."
> (see Catalogue 1989, p.153).

This canto had previously been illustrated by Botticelli, whose Matelda bears some resemblance to Leonardo's figure in her movement.[8] Whether or not Leonardo's drawing specifically illustrates Dante's description, there is little doubt that she represents Leonardo's version of the *donna honesta*, the ideally virtuous woman, as outlined in his Notebooks and as built into contemporary culture. Indeed, the text and the drawing may be seen to be connected in other, more general ways, since Dante's image of female beauty undoubtedly rebounded on 15th- and 16th-century notions of decorous behaviour. Contemporary dance manuals, for example, repeatedly make the point that, when dancing, women should take almost undiscernible steps, keeping their legs and feet close together. Here again, Leonardo's moving figure is not a simple copy of a natural pose - a matter of straightforward empirical observation, even though it may have been taken from a model, and even though the final impression is one of a disarming lifelikeness. Rather, it is life, or nature, filtered through a prism of convention - a complex combination of observation with literary, social and moral ideals.

In pointing out the conventional basis of many of Leonardo's moving figures - and I stress the word basis here - my aim has not been to undermine his originality, or the extent of his innovation. That originality was overwhelmingly evident in the exhibition and also forms the *leitmotif* of most writing on the artist - so much so that it would almost have been superfluous to rehearse the point again. My aim has been rather to place that originality within a context, so that we may see Leonardo not as a solitary and isolated genius, in a way which renders him impenetrable and remote, but as an artist working within the conventions and limitations of his time, however much he may ultimately have transformed them. The opening caption to the exhibition made the following claim:

> "In spite of the great range of his activities, it was Leonardo's work as an artist that shaped his career."

I would suggest, in conclusion, that we may reverse that equation and say that it was Leonardo's career as an artist that shaped his work.

Sharon Fermor

---

[8] See K. Clark, *The Drawings by Sandro Botticelli for Dante's Divine Comedy*, London 1976, pp.142-5.

# Leonardo and the helix

There was a section in the Hayward Gallery exhibition entitled 'The Vortex'. It is here that this discussion will start; and it will go further than is possible within the limitations of any exhibition in exploring Leonardo's interest not only in the vortex but rather, in more general terms, in the helix and in helical movements, and in considering the implications of these for the development of his figure-style.

"The vortex... becomes a ubiquitous sign of the life beneath the surface of nature", wrote Martin Kemp (Catalogue 1989, p.118); and this rightly conveys the notion that the vortex is a dynamic force - a power which may be small but continuous, or may be sudden, short-term but cataclysmic. These opposing aspects of vortexes are well illustrated by two drawings in that section in the exhibition, the eddies of water pushing against a breakwater (62), which already hint at the inherent power of water available to be harnessed for mechanical purposes, and the fantastical visions of natural disaster in Leonardo's deluge studies (63) where the vast whirls of force break rocks asunder and blow aside the foreground trees.

My concise dictionary defines 'vortex' as 'a whirlpool; a whirling mass; anything which engulfs or absorbs'. A helix, on the other hand, is defined as 'a spiral, anything coiled': this term I take to include the elemental forces of the vortex, but to extend beyond these to embrace all spiralling, corkscrew forms whether in movement or static, whether exerting force or representing contained, rhythmic tensions.

Leonardo identified helical forms and movements in almost all facets of the natural world; and one suspects that he came instinctively, sub-consciously perhaps, to believe that spiral shapes underlie many of the principal, primary forms of nature, not least organic mechanisms. He might have found this belief confirmed, had he known about the double helix of the DNA molecule, the 'messenger' which conveys individual information from cell to cell in the growth of each organic form and species.

Examples of his fascination with helical growth or movement can be found throughout his writings and drawings relating to his scientific explorations. We will also see that this form of movement was endemic in his thoughts about mechanics and the machines he designed. Consideration of these two aspects of his concern with the helix forms the basis of the examination, towards the end of this lecture, of Leonardo's recognition and exploration of two literally vital aspects of the human figure, the compact, spring-like power inherent in a pose of vigorous torsion, and the contained rhythms of a fluently twisting pose which imply smooth movement or readiness to move, thus adding a lively spontaneity to painted or drawn figures.

The sheet showing a pensive old man in profile apparently deep in his thoughts about the movement of water around obstacles (21) has a keen if coincidental appropriateness in this context. It is clear from the fold in the page that the sheet was originally bound into a notebook, and the drawings on the two halves of the sheet were not drawn together and were never intended to be seen together. Yet we appear to have a fortuitous insight into Leonardo's obsession with the movements of water, and the power inherent in those movements. So the first aspect of helical movement to be considered is where it is connected with power: what Leonardo called the 'prime mover', the power inherent in nature. Water is perhaps the obvious example, which Leonardo explored at great length.

Leonardo's observations that water often tends to move round obstructions in a helical pattern, or - in the case of the carefully detailed and finely observed pattern created by water plunging from a conduit into a pool (**61**) - sets up complex swirling eddies, may have stimulated him to consider more extensively the applications of the helix in harnessing power and developing useful work from the 'prime mover'. So the studies of water in movement can be seen to lead to the study of the application of the helix; and the intermediary here may perhaps have been Leonardo's interest in the Archimedes Screw. This is best illustrated in an early drawing (Calder 1970, p.127) which shows two types of Archimedes Screw alongside another device for raising water based on the principle of the water wheel.

The principle of the Archimedes Screw is that water will run down into a hollow corkscrew tube when this is turned on its axis, so that gradually the water in the tube will be wound upwards, to flow into a tank at the top of the screw. This has obvious applications for water storage and distribution systems, for irrigation purposes, domestic or industrial uses, and so on. Early in his scientific work, Leonardo also held out the pious, naïve hope that he might use this principle in designing a perpetual motion machine (**59**). The idea here was that the power needed to screw the water up the inner spiral tube would be provided by the centrifugal, circular force generated by water flowing down the outer spiral tube. The constant movement of water up and down would be self-perpetuating, and the water running out at the bottom would serve as a source of hydraulic energy. Needless to say, this could not work; and only a few years later Leonardo himself was pouring scorn on the notion of perpetual motion.

The helical movement of the screw has a wide range of mechanical applications. Two examples of rather primitive machines, designed early in Leonardo's career in the 1480s, respectively perhaps shortly before and shortly after he moved to Milan to work for Lodovico Sforza, are an automatic file-engraver (Kemp 1981, pl.32) and a giant crossbow (CA, f.53v-b; Popham 1946, pl.302). In the first, the source of power is a weight: its descent turns an axle which drives both a screw, which moves the block carrying the file slowly along, and the sharp-ended hammer that engraves the grooves. In the second, a fearsome if somewhat fantastically huge machine of war, the crossbow string is drawn back by manual winding of a long screw.

Another impressive invention for military application, again bearing out Leonardo's promise in the famous letter of about 1482 to Lodovico Sforza of his ability as a military engineer, uses both the screw and a series of worm gears (CA, f.2r-a; Popham 1946, pl.319). This is again an early design, with the machine parts rather strung out, and not built into the sort of compact mechanism of Leonardo's mature systems. Its purpose was to exert a varying compressing force on the longitudinal section of a cannon barrel which is drawn forward using a turning screw, so as to press it into the required thickness which varies along its length. The machine is powered by water, using the principle of the propeller in reverse - a fan wheel which transfers water power into rotary power. The work efficiency of this power is increased greatly by a series of worm-and-cog gears, by which the corkscrew movement of the worm turns a toothed wheel - another application of helical movement which Leonardo used in the hoist mechanism design constructed as a model in the exhibition (**122** and **fig.53**).

In these machine designs, we can see how Leonardo explored the possibilities of using turning spirals to transfer power from one axis to another, and to increase force and hence the work efficiency of his machines. Indeed, in the gun-barrel drawing he added a calculation of the power ratios developed: each transfer from worm to gearwheel provides a 12-fold increase in force, so that starting with a notional power of 1000 units he ended up with 20,736,000 units.

Another source of power that Leonardo investigated is that with which the helix itself can be invested, the contained power of the twisted, wound spring. In two beautiful drawings he explored the application of that energy, and the problems associated with the spring as a source of power. One (**ill.B** on p.81) is the earliest known representation of the wheel-lock: here, the tensed, coiled-steel spring is shown by Leonardo in three dimensions with loving clarity and finesse.[1] Heavy parallel hatching explores deep into the cylinder which holds the spring, and the coils of thick steel are defined by touches of curvilinear hatching of the sort that we find exploited extensively in the drawings for the *Leda and the Swan* (**14**, **75**) in the first years of the new century.

Similar 'bracelet' hatching indicates the roundness of the cylinder which contains the powerful clock spring in the marvellously inventive drawing (**116**, **right**) for an equalising device to compensate for the gradual loss of power as the spring unwinds. Although the spring itself is hidden from view, we can imagine the corkscrew movement of the wonderful toothed volute as it is turned by the uncoiling spring, and as the lantern gear is in turn revolved as it rises up the volute gradient. To judge from the exact and full detail of Leonardo's record of his invention, the play of these interlocking spiral movements built into a neat, compact mechanism gave him great satisfaction -

---

[1] For discussion of this mechanism, see Reti ed.1974, pp.182-3 and pl.183/2.

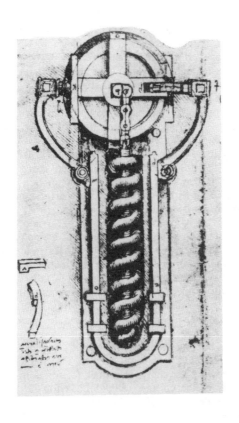

**ill.B**  Leonardo da Vinci, *Design for a wheel-lock.*
Milan, Ambrosiana, detail of CA, f.56vb.

even though the mechanism could not work if constructed precisely to this
design.

We have looked at a number of examples of Leonardo's grasp of the value
of harnessed water-power and spring-power for driving machines: he also
investigated aerodynamic power, and designed mechanisms driven by this
'prime mover'. An ingenious roasting-spit driven by the power of the hot air
rising from the cooking fire beneath appears in one of his earliest mechanical
drawings, of about 1480, in the Codex Atlanticus (Reti ed. 1974, pl.175/1;
Calder 1970, p.106). The bigger the fire and the more intense the heat,

Leonardo observed, the faster the 'propeller' will be driven round and the meat will be turned. If this mechanism looks closer to Heath Robinson than to the complex, automated machines that Leonardo designed later, the reverse process appears in a mature drawing of great neatness and simplicity (Calder 1970, p.226). A propeller is driven by a tightly coiled spring so that the device rises into the air: this anticipates the principle of the helicopter, even if it is only the design of a 'whirlibird' toy. "I find", wrote Leonardo "that if this instrument be well made... and be turned swiftly, the propeller will make its spiral in the air and will rise high..." (MS B, f.83v). This helical propulsion to generate air-borne flight in turn finds its reflection in Leonardo's investigations into the flight paths of birds: "the rising of birds without beating their wings is due solely to their circular motion within the motion of the wind" (CA, f.308r-b) he wrote alongside a diagrammatic sketch (Keele 1983, fig.6.35) of birds rising along a helical line.

Given the importance of the screw, the worm-gear and the spring, and of the helical movements of all these machine elements, in Leonardo's mechanical designs of the 1480s and 1490s, it is hardly surprising to find that the way he drew to record, and even to reconstruct, the natural movements of a wide range of different living organisms often falls into spiral patterns. This is true not only of merely diagrammatic representations like the sketch of bird-flight but also of such examples as the illustration of blood moving through the valves of the heart, flowing in minute whorls shown by fine curvilinear pen-lines (55).

But we also find elaborate helical curvilinearity exploited by Leonardo in fully evolved records of natural form, such as the Star of Bethlehem (57), perhaps his best-known plant study, or studies for forms in paintings, such as the celebrated study of the coiffure (58) of Leda for the lost *Leda and the Swan*. In the plant drawing, Leonardo appears to 'correct' the inevitable imperfections of Nature in his wish to assert the primacy of the helix: the plant's leaves flow out from a central core to generate a rhythmic wave pattern of spiral movement which almost encourages the observer to read the plant as having the potential of animal movement, or as though at any moment it might take off like the 'whirlibird' toy helicopter. Likewise, in defining Leda's hair almost strand by strand, Leonardo delighted in contrasting the free-flowing hairs pulled through the centre of the plaits with the tightly plaited tresses pinned up into a conical helix, reminiscent in shape of the toothed volute of the clock-spring equalising device.

In his treatise *On Painting* (1435) Leon Battista Alberti had already written: "movements are especially pleasing in hair where part of it spirals as if wishing to knot itself, waves in the air like flames, twines around itself like a serpent, while part rises here, part there;"[2] and Leonardo himself later drew

---

[2] Leon Battista Alberti *On Painting*, trans. J.R. Spencer, New Haven 1956, p.81.

a direct parallel between such plaiting and the movement of water: "Observe the motion of the surface of water, which resembles the behaviour of hair which has two motions, of which one depends on the weight of the strands, the other on the line of its revolving just as water makes revolving eddies..." (Windsor 12579; see Clark/Pedretti 1968, p.113; and cf. Catalogue 1989, p.124).

We have seen in some detail how helical movements and the movements of helixes absorbed Leonardo's attention in his studies and in his inventions. In his investigations into human movements too, he recognised the potential of twisting poses both for recording the natural movements of man and for communicating forceful expressive ideas, such as vigour, ferocity, sensuality, readiness for action, and many others.

In a long series of descriptions of 'movements of man' Leonardo wrote of a man preparing to throw a stone:

> "Having twisted and moved himself towards the other side, where he prepares for the application of his power, he pivots with speed and convenience towards the point at which he wishes to release the stone from his hands..." (Kemp/Walker 1989, p.143);

and 'on undulating movements (serpeggiare) and balance in figures and other animals' he wrote:

> "When representing a human figure or some graceful animal, be careful to avoid a wooden stiffness; that is to say make them move with equipoise and balance so as not to look like a piece of wood; but those you want to represent as strong you must not make so, excepting in the turn of the head." (Richter 1970, I pp.343-4).

These ideas are well realised in a drawing of a twisting man seen from the front and back (**plate 17**). This can be compared with the drawing by Pollaiuolo, for which he was already celebrated in his lifetime, of a 'Nude man seen from front, side and back' (Paris, Louvre 1486), but which shows a difference in conception of the pose. Leonardo recognised both an inherent tendency in the human figure to take up spiral poses, and the value of studying this from two viewpoints; Pollaiuolo, always fascinated by the pivoting figure and concerned to record its three-dimensional form in two dimensions, worked with a simpler pose which does not twist through space.

In his anatomical dissection studies of the shoulder (**95, 96**), Leonardo moved round the corpse to draw and redraw the form in order to come to a fuller understanding of its three-dimensionality. On the second of these sheets he explained in a detailed note, and with the help of a stellate diagram, how he selected his points of view (see Catalogue 1989, pp.172-3). Like the 'nude man from front and back' sketches, the shoulder dissection studies illustrate Leonardo's observations that:

"One and the same action will show itself as infinitely varied because it may be seen from an infinite number of locations. These locations have continuous quantity, and continuous quantity is infinitely divisible. Hence from varied viewpoints each human action is displayed as infinite in itself." (Kemp/Walker 1989, p.133)

What we have in these drawings is not so much a spiral pose as a spiralling draughtsman: Leonardo himself moved around the form he drew just as the nude man in Windsor 12631v twists and turns around a vertical axis. Movement of this sort was not unusual in later 15th-century Florentine art: a good parallel to Leonardo's drawing is Bertoldo di Giovanni's small bronze of *Apollo* (Pope-Hennessy 1971, pl.91) cast sometime perhaps in the later 1480s. Free-standing bronzes such as this one were intended to be admired from many angles, either by being set in the centre of a table around which the observer could move, or by being picked up and pivoted in the hands. This way of using bronzes must have encouraged sculptors to explore complex poses, so Leonardo was by no means original or unique in his enthusiasm for human helical movements.

Likewise, a parallel may be drawn between Leonardo's portrait of *Cecilia Gallerani* (**fig.26**), the 'Lady with an Ermine', dating from about 1485, and Verrocchio's bronze *Putto with a Dolphin* (Pope-Hennessy 1971, pl.78) possibly already cast by the time that Leonardo joined the sculptor's workshop. What is interesting, though, is the rapid maturing of Leonardo's interest in such poses, and the range of his exploitation of their expressive potential. If we look at a sheet of figure drawings of ca.1480 (**7**), associated with the preparation of the unfinished Uffizi *Adoration of the Magi* (**fig.16**), we sense that the twisting figure up at the top left hand corner is a chance example of a helical pose: Leonardo was at this stage concentrating attention on more planar movements and poses in all the other studies on this sheet. But on the splendid sheet of various studies in the Turin Royal Library (**plate 16**) which aptly exemplifies the range of Leonardo's mature interests, we see juxtaposed with sketches for the *Battle of Anghiari* in around 1503-4 two studies of fully-modelled twisting figures. Paying these much more attention than the other studies on the sheet, Leonardo described the musculature in torsion in great detail as though preoccupied with the analysis of the contained power of the model's pose.

Similarly, we can compare a relatively early drawing of *St Sebastian* (**plate 18**), perhaps one of eight versions of the subject listed in a memorandum of the mid 1480s (Kemp/Walker 1989, pp.263-4), with a standard Florentine representation, such as Botticelli's Berlin *St Sebastian* painted a decade or so earlier. The pose of Botticelli's figure is planar, uncomplicated; Leonardo's is almost aggressively twisting, the left knee thrown across the right leg, the torso in strained curvature, the head sharply twisted back against the movement of the shoulders. Very much the same pose, for very much the same expressive purposes, was later used (in reverse) by Michelangelo in the *Rebellious Slave* for the Julius II monument, and now in Paris.

This is a significant indication of the fact that Leonardo was exploring ideas about spiralling poses some decades before Michelangelo began to develop the vocabulary of poses which led to the mid 16th-century theory of the *figura serpentinata* epitomised by Lomazzo:

> "the greatest grace and loveliness that a figure may have is that it seems to move itself;... to represent this movement no form is more suited than a flame of fire... that represents the tortuosity of a live serpent when it moves, which is the property of a flame of fire that undulates."[3]

Leonardo himself wrote 'Of pictures in outline' that:

> "the contours of any object should be considered with the most careful attention, observing how they twist like a serpent."[4]

This advice immediately brings to mind not only Leonardo's own drawings of dragons (84), but also the marvellous black chalk study (71) for the drawing of *Neptune* presented to Antonio Segni in 1502, in which the sea-horses coil and twist with extraordinary dynamic urgency.

Leonardo's most extensive consideration of serpentinate figures was associated with the **Trivulzio Monument** planned in Milan between about 1508 and 1512. The chained captives which were to have been set at the corners of the base of this monument have inevitably been compared with Michelangelo's *Slaves* for the Julius II monument of the middle of the second decade. They can be seen in the sketches for the **Trivulzio Monument**, notably in Windsor 12355 (Clark/Pedretti 1968, pp.43-4; Popham 1946, pl.91) but also in (16); and it is evident that to provide energetic figures which would look effective from a range of viewpoints, powerfully coiled poses in full torsion with tensed, firmly built muscles are ideal - even more so, indeed, than in the caryatid-like figures set against the pilaster-herms of Michelangelo's monument design. Just as the earlier St Sebastian drawing can be compared with the *Rebellious Slave*, so also another drawing (ill.C) best

---

[3] Cited by D. Summers, *Michelangelo and the Language of Art*, Princeton 1981, pp.81-2.

[4] ibid., pp.82-3.

associated with the *Trivulzio Monument* project appears similar in pose to the *Slave* seen in reverse. Given Leonardo's earlier enthusiasm for this sort of pose, it seems likely that his ideas about the embryonic *figura serpentinata* foreshadow Michelangelo's Julius Tomb *Slaves*.

The final example of Leonardo's helical figures brings us back to a design referred to earlier, the *Leda and the Swan*, probably started around 1505. Although to judge from copies of the finished painting (**fig.31**), itself now sadly lost, it did not show the extensiveness of spiralling movement of other figure designs by Leonardo in these years, it was nonetheless a celebrated and often reflected prototype for sinuous elegance of pose, even if not for energetic twist. In exactly what way the standing *Leda* evolved from the series of studies for a 'Kneeling Leda' is not clear; but these studies show Leonardo's inventive experimentation with a helical pose based ultimately on classical figures such as the *Crouching Venus* (London, British Museum) once at Urbino, and at this time owned by Cesare Borgia. On an intriguing sheet of studies (**74**) associated with the preparation of the *Battle of Anghiari* in about 1505, Leonardo tried out a series of ideas for the figure of Leda in minute sketches. These matured into the progressively larger and more fully calculated drawings in Rotterdam (**14**) and Chatsworth (**75**), in which the corkscrew movement of Leda's rising pose is emphasised by the curvilinear outlines of the swan's wings and the flexing of his neck, to develop rhythmic spiral movements reminiscent of the tails of the sea-horses in the drawing (**71**) for Antonio Segni's *Neptune*. These fluent, helical movements are further stressed by the highly developed 'bracelet' hatching, already seen on the clock-spring equalising mechanism drawing (**116, right**). Using this method of linear modelling, Leonardo generated sensuously full forms for Leda's breasts, thighs and calves, and these are again reinforced by the similar treatment of the swan's torso and neck. Leonardo used the same means of stressing both plumpness of form and helically twisting and turning movements in his pen redrawing of the quick black chalk sketches of a child on a sheet of studies (**29**) probably for a *Virgin and Child with St Anne* composition of a few years later.

We may guess that the 'bracelet' hatching technique was further exploited, for the same purposes of stressing sensuous, rounded forms, in drawings for the *Standing Leda*, now known only through copies, since in his copy drawing of this figure Raphael interpreted Leda's forms in just the same manner.[5] That this figure entered and remained firmly in Raphael's consciousness is indicated by his later reuses of the helical motif, notably in his *Galatea*; and it seems likely too that Michelangelo had not entirely

---

[5] For Raphael's copy (Windsor 12759), see P. Joannides, *The Drawings of Raphael*, Oxford 1983, no.98, p.156; and *Drawings by Raphael*, exhibition catalogue, London (British Museum) 1983, no.40, pp.61-2.

**ill.C** Leonardo da Vinci, *Nude male with hands bound to column.*
Windsor, Royal Library, 12583A.
Red chalk, with pen and ink, on pink paper; 110 x 68 mm.

forgotten the figure when he came to carve his Sta Maria sopra Minerva
*Risen Christ* many years later. Such profound tributes as Raphael's and
Michelangelo's to Leonardo's **Standing Leda** can seldom have been paid by
two major artists to the conception of a great painter of the generation earlier.
The easy, sensuous grace of pose, that quality of the inherent vitality of inner
life that Leonardo captured, and to which Raphael strongly responded in his
copy, was the logical conclusion of Leonardo's concentrated investigations
during his first Milanese period into the issue of spiral movement. This he
came to see as a pattern frequently adopted by Nature herself both for sources
of power and for the movements, positions and growth shapes of organic
forms. No wonder then that the helix, in all its vital manifestations,
preoccupied Leonardo throughout his career, and that its contained life-
rhythms pervade his figure-style in the works of art of his maturity.

Francis Ames-Lewis

# Leonardo and architecture

Hundreds of drawings survive to show that many aspects of architecture fascinated Leonardo; copious notes and diagrams about ideal towns with subterranean waterways, drawings of palaces and villas, houses and stables, diagrams of the ways in which arches break under strain, of temporary wooden structures and architectural machines.[1] His abilities as a mapper of towns and canals, his knowledge of surveying, of triangulation and architectural devices, is not open to question. Leonardo clearly knew everything you needed to know about structure and design in an age of primitive technology. Yet when we examine his career as an architect and compare him with his contemporaries like Bramante, Amadeo, Giuliano da Sangallo or Francesco di Giorgio, we see that they are as different as chalk from cheese. Not only is the documentation about Leonardo's life and architecture entirely different from that for other architects, but his drawings are too; he does not have the same interests, he does not draw in the same way or for the same reasons. Here we shall outline these differences, then seek to explain them with the help of some ill-advised and no doubt foolhardy generalisations.

Our first observations are disconcerting: (1) not one building designed by Leonardo survives; and (2) we cannot prove that any project in Italy or France was intended to have been built entirely under his supervision and exclusively to his design. What then do the documents tell us of Leonardo's life and architecture?

Like everybody else in the Renaissance above a very low economic level, architects appeared in legal documents. Almost everybody had, from time to time, to carry out legal transactions - such as paying and receiving rent, buying land and houses, paying debts and so on. Thus, there is a superabundance of material about the architect Amadeo, Leonardo's contemporary in Milan, involving his houses and land, tenants, creditors, debtors, clothes, apprenticeships and co-operatives with other sculptors and engineers. But in Leonardo's case, there exist no legal documents, except those for the *Virgin of the Rocks* (figs.23-24), about this kind of activity in Milan. Indeed, Leonardo's Will confirms that the only land he owned at his death was the vineyard given to him by Lodovico il Moro in 1498, and a small property inherited later from his father in Fiesole; and the only bank-account he maintained consistently throughout his life was at the Ospedale di Sta Maria Nuova in Florence, to which he sent money from Milan and Rome

---

[1] I would like to stress that this account is provisional, but while it will undoubtedly change in detail, I think that the main points will remain. I hope to publish it in fuller form soon. To the full bibliography in Pedretti 1986 should now be added the recent essay by J. Guillaume in *Leonardo architect and engineer*, Montreal 1987, which is well-informed, up-to-date and, in my view, appropriately sceptical.

after 1499. Like Bramante, therefore, Leonardo had no need of these standard legal processes, and the reason is almost certainly that he was supported by wealthy patrons. In Milan, that patron was certainly the Duke in the 1490s, most of whose private correspondence and account-books have been lost, whence the remarkably poor documentation of Leonardo during his Milanese period. And later in life, there are indications of stipends from Cesare Borgia, the French in Milan and France, and the Pope in Rome.

But if the documentation about Leonardo's life is thin, that concerning his career as an architect is almost invisible. There are, of course, a number of general allusions in the 16th century by Vasari, Cellini and others to Leonardo's expertise in architecture, but if we look at the contemporary material, a very curious picture starts to emerge: only four contemporary sources before 1502 say that he was an architect or engineer; and throughout his life, whenever he is given a title, he is almost invariably called 'painter'. It is true that in the celebrated letter to the Duke of Milan of about 1482, Leonardo commends himself as an architect by saying that in time of peace he can give perfect satisfaction in architecture and in the composition of public and private buildings: yet that claim is the tenth and penultimate item in the letter, coming after siege devices, naval weapons, mortars, military mining, armoured cars and so on. The famous Milanese document of the 1490s, which lists ducal and communal engineers, as well as Amadeo, Bramante, Dolcebuono and Leonardo under a different heading, was published in a scrambled form, so that Leonardo was put in the wrong category. The heading under which Leonardo appeared is at the top of the *verso*, but it is mutilated, leaving only the adjective 'descripti', without a noun. The result is that whatever Leonardo was being described as, it was neither as a ducal nor as a communal engineer. Leonardo is also described as an engineer when he visited the Duomo di Pavia in 1490, but the epithet is almost certainly *ad hoc* - i.e. it describes what he was doing at that moment without implying continuous or habitual, paid service as an engineer at Pavia or anywhere else. In 1502 Cesare Borgia described him as his 'beloved architect and engineer', but the reference was to Leonardo as a military architect (or rather draughtsman), because the letter was a safe-conduct allowing him to go anywhere in Cesare's territories in order to inspect forts and their sites. In 1506, Charles d'Amboise, when writing to the Florentines, remarked generally that Leonardo was famous as a painter, but that it is not as well known that he was good at designing and architecture. Charles also says that Leonardo had worked satisfactorily in this field for him, but does not tell us in what sense. The first unequivocal reference to Leonardo as an architect was in 1507, when Robertet wrote to the Florentines from Milan saying that he is "our painter and ingenieur ordinaire". And that is almost the sum of specific references to Leonardo as an architect in contemporary sources.

But Leonardo appears extraordinarily rarely in any other architectural documents, and then only with a minute array of the architect's standard skills. Architects like Giuliano, Bramante and Amadeo appear in architectural documents in a great number of roles: they were appointed as engineers to building projects, they appear in contracts with patrons and stone-masons, as witnesses to sub-contracts, as advising experts, as makers of templates, models and drawings. They also appear in the account books of institutions such as churches, hospitals or palaces, receiving payments for various architectural duties. Some 1,100 documents record in grinding detail Amadeo's activities for the Duomo in Milan, his salary, his estimates of stone and land, his property, his models and drawings. So too elsewhere Luca Fancelli refers to the designs that Alberti has sent him; Francesco di Giorgio is contracted to make a model for the Calcinaio in Cortona; Brunelleschi appears innumerable times in the minutes of the Duomo in Florence; and so on *ad infinitum*.

Leonardo is totally different: he was never appointed as the supervising architect of a church; he never drew a salary from a church or from any other institution. There is no proof that he was a ducal engineer or that he ever directed a building project. He only appeared three times as an adviser - a very common duty for other architects - in the planning of a project: for the cupola of Milan Cathedral, for the Duomo di Pavia, and for S. Salvatore al Monte in Florence. With the sole exception of the cupola of Milan Cathedral, there was no occasion in the whole of his career when he was documented as having made models, drawings or templates for any kind of structure. And even in the few cases where Leonardo did work at an architectural project it is usually difficult to establish his role precisely. We may mention briefly three cases. First, Leonardo was paid for a model for the cupola of Milan Cathedral between 1487 and 1490, and a number of his drawings for the project survive. The famous sectional drawing from the Codex Atlanticus was presumably the basis for the model itself (Pedretti 1986, pl.39): yet it was unbuildable, combining a traditional Lombard octagon with a Brunelleschian double-shell that was patently absurd, since the static advantages of the square-based vault were negated by the extra weight of the structurally disadvantageous octagon. When the cupola was built, not one of Leonardo's structural suggestions was accepted, nor was he employed by the Duomo in any capacity except a temporary one. Moreover, when Leonardo wrote a brief account of the problems of building the vault, he did not address the matter in any detail, but rather rewrote a passage from Galen which said that buildings could be ill and needed the attention of doctor-architects.

Second, a now famous project may be nothing more than wishful thinking by Professor Pedretti: a sheet in the Codex Atlanticus (Pedretti 1986, pls.369-70) is said to be a plan drawn up by Leonardo, possibly in conjunction with Pope Leo X in 1515, to transform the area between S. Lorenzo and S. Marco in Florence, at about the time that the competition for the new façade of S. Lorenzo was getting under way. The same project is, it is held, shown in the Book of Hours of Laodomia de'Medici in the British Museum dated to between 1502 and 1517. It is alleged that part of the project was to build a gigantic palace shown on the same sheet next to the existing Palazzo Medici. Nothing happened: no documents mention any such intention on the part of Leo X, though it is not impossible; neither the manuscript illustration nor the drawing need be dated to 1515, or connected with each other; nor is it clear that Leonardo's sketch is anything but a rapid, therefore inaccurate sketch of part of the town made for no particular reason, or rather, for a reason that we do not know. It is not clear why it should have entered anybody's head to build such a huge extra palace next to the existing Palazzo Medici; or indeed, why the little sketch of a palace should be associated with the urban plan; or, finally, why either the palace or the street-plan should be connected with the details of an elevation on the same sheet. The result of all this is that the evidence is not strong enough to prove that Leonardo was making a project for the restructuring of Florence.

Third, there is conversely no doubt that Leonardo made drawings for a palace at Romorantin in 1517, but we have not the faintest idea how to evaluate his contribution to the project, since it was abandoned just after it was begun. For one thing, there are practically no contemporary French records or drawings of any kind, so the contributions of local architects remain unknown. For another, Leonardo's drawings are mainly small-scale sketches of grand schemes, with, it seems, only one drawing (of uncertain date) of the elevation as a whole. But, as is frequently the case with Leonardo's project drawings, there are practically none that can be proved to illustrate details - such as entablatures, columns, capitals, bases, or pilasters. So one may guess that Leonardo was never involved beyond the general, initial planning stage (Pedretti 1986, pls.392-3 and 395-400).

So much, then, for a rapid examination of what the documents do not say about Leonardo as architect. What in general can we learn from the drawings? Just as Leonardo does not appear in the documents as other builders do, so too his drawings have a number of characteristics that are entirely different from theirs. We shall argue that not only did Leonardo have little interest in Vitruvius, Alberti or the antique, but that he was only fitfully concerned even with contemporary architecture or style.

Despite immensely different linguistic abilities, Alberti, Filarete, Francesco di Giorgio and Giuliano da Sangallo all shared an obsession with the antique, not only as they knew about it from Vitruvius (whom Alberti alone could read properly), but also as they could see it and recreate it in drawings. Francesco di Giorgio, for example, tried endlessly to translate Vitruvius and illustrate what he said; and naturally he was fascinated by the antique buildings themselves. He travelled ceaselessly to Rome; he drew the plans of the ruins; he recreated elevations; he carefully labelled the buildings with their names; he copied details of entablatures, bases and capitals; he wanted to know the correct terms and forms for all parts of the orders. So too Giuliano da Sangallo. Both these architects had started their intense study of antique theory and practice in the 1460s; Alberti and Filarete started studying the antique long before and had written up their treatises by 1452 and 1463/4 respectively. By the early 16th century, and Leonardo's eventual arrival in Rome, Bramante's and Raphael's synthetic classicism - in part direct quotation, but mostly adaptation of antique forms - was in full swing.

Yet how did Leonardo respond to Vitruvius and the antique? We know that he owned a book of drawings of antique buildings and a copy of Alberti's treatise, but there are only about three occasions when he adapted ideas from the architectural parts of that text. His indifference to Vitruvius was similar: there appear to be just two occasions on which he sought to visualise Vitruvian architectural details, once in an illustration of an Ionic capital and once in a labelled drawing of the details of a base (Pedretti 1986, pls.70-1). During his Milanese period Leonardo's lack of interest extended not just to the texts about ancient architecture, but also - selectively - to the physical remains: there is a scattering of drawings of Early Christian structures, such as Sta Maria in Pertica in Pavia and S. Sepolcro, S. Lorenzo and S. Satiro in Milan (Pedretti 1986, pls.25-6 and 436-7). He drew their plans in many variations, but the impression in all cases is that he was not interested in them as manifestations of antique style or structure, since he rarely made separate drawings of details or elevations, but rather as patterns for ideal centralised plans upon which to make endless elaborations. Leonardo's opportunities in his Milanese period to study the antique were relatively limited, but he seems still to have been practically comatose with respect to architecture when he got to Rome, where his apparent indifference to antique architecture is astonishing. The splendours of the Arch of Constantine, the Theatre of Marcellus, the Colosseum, the Pantheon, the Temple of Vesta at Tivoli and so on, which had assumed the status of holy writ for Bramante and Raphael, left him unmoved. We know that he went to Tivoli, yet apparently he left no drawings of any part of Hadrian's Villa; nor do copies of any of these buildings or even parts of them survive except very rarely; nor does he mention them in the notebooks. From these, we know merely that he visited Civitavecchia, since he left a little sketch of the port (Pedretti 1986, pl.359) apparently reconstructing the imperial palace there, as well as a detailed verbal description of the antique brick-work; and that he went to S. Paolo fuori le Mura and, it seems, measured it.

Leonardo's interest in contemporary architecture was also strangely patchy, especially in his Roman period. It is true that in the *Adoration* of 1481 he copied the flights of stairs inside S. Miniato al Monte (Pedretti 1986, pl.405). Otherwise from Florence he recorded only the plans of S. Spirito and the Angeli (Pedretti 1986, pl.81); but like a needle stuck in a groove, he remained obsessed by Brunelleschi's cupola and the octagon of the Angeli and used them long after he had left Florence and had become acquainted with the majestic hemispheres of Sta Maria delle Grazie in Milan and the Pantheon in Rome. He only occasionally drew details and adaptations of contemporary buildings and he rarely copied complete plans; he never reproduced complete elevations. For example, he made variants of the plan of the Duomo di Pavia (Pedretti 1986, pl.30); he drew only the lower exterior profiles and a minute version of the plan of the Grazie (Pedretti 1986, pls.112-6); and he drew merely a part of the stairway and a part of the Cappella del Perdono in the palace at Urbino (Pedretti 1986, pls.247-8). And his response to Bramante and Raphael in Rome is equally puzzling: one drawing (Pedretti 1986, pl.253) may be a version of the outside of the Chigi stables; another (Pedretti 1986, pl.308), apparently incorporates the coupled columns of Bramante's House of Raphael; a third (Pedretti 1986, pl.348) may be a version of a bay of the Belvedere; a fourth (Pedretti 1986, pl.178), perhaps triggered by the discovery of an Etruscan tomb in 1507, takes Bramante's *Tempietto* (or Francesco di Giorgio's peripteral structures in the Turin Codex) and fits it with the steps of the roof of the Pantheon. And that is more or less the whole of Leonardo's response to the greatest explosion of *all'antica* building in the history of architecture.

Leonardo's drawings present us, on the one hand, with myriad details of buildings, and, on the other hand, with grand schemes drawn on a small scale, almost always without accompanying detailed drawings to convince us that he was producing a project which builders could follow. On practically no occasion is an overall scheme, like that for the Villa of Mariolo Guiscardi, the Villa at Vaprio d'Adda, or Romorantin (Pedretti 1986, pls.87-8, 331-8 and 392-400 respectively), combined with illustrations of the details of such structures, such as elevations, wall-thicknesses, pilasters, capitals, cornices, and so on. And it is extraordinarily rare for Leonardo to label a drawing - the only two in MS.B are the versions of S. Sepolcro in Milan and of Sta Maria in Pertica in Pavia - and even rarer for him to produce a scale drawing: there survive only two. Clearly this is in total contrast to the project drawings of Giuliano da Sangallo, which are drawn to scale in plan and labelled, with dimensions, for presentation to the patron. In sum, these observations, though sweeping and unlikely to be true for all cases, lead to one conclusion: Leonardo's project drawings were merely first general thoughts and never got to the stage required for detailed presentation. This reinforces the impression that even if Leonardo had made major contributions to the initial planning of any project, it is not likely that his involvement went any further in any case.

If no building designed by Leonardo survives; if we cannot guarantee that he was responsible for any projected building; if he was comparatively uninterested in the antique, and only fitfully interested in contemporary architecture and in the most up-to-date styles; what then remains? A central fact, revealed by the documents, is that his livelihood did not depend on architecture, but rather - one guesses - on painting, for which there are contracts and other documents, stage scenery, costume design, perhaps mechanical devices, but especially on making maps of canals, towns and drawings of fortifications for strategic purposes. His interest in architecture was spasmodic, occurring particularly in the 1480s, and thereafter sporadically, with a flourish in the 1510s in Florence, a little in Rome, and more in France at the end of his life.

But we can derive some other generalisations particularly from MS.B of the 1480s, the largest collection of designs from the whole of his career. All the negatives isolated above are represented here. Furthermore, another of Leonardo's stranger characteristics is well represented by MS.B, his habitual lurches between the daringly up-to-date and the inexplicably old-fashioned: thus his advanced-looking centralized or mixed plans are often little more than versions of S. Lorenzo or S. Satiro crowned with Brunelleschi's cupola. He also used the by then old-fashioned Florentine biforate window with tracery in his famous stable study, and later in a version of a bay from Bramante's *Belvedere*, and elsewhere (Pedretti 1986, pls.354 and 356). In sum: his Florentine past stayed with him throughout his Milanese period, and his Milanese period stayed with him into his Roman period in much the same way. This is Leonardo's 'chain-thinking': a process of catenation by which he seized on certain motifs early in life, and chased them through to the end. Just as certain poses originating in the late Florentine series of drawings for the *Virgin and Child with a Cat* (e.g. **6**) return again and again even as late as the *Virgin, Child, St Anne and a Lamb* (**fig. 29**) so also Brunelleschi's cupola stuck, as did the plans of S. Lorenzo and S. Satiro in Milan, to be endlessly repeated and varied even in his late architectural sketches.

Leonardo's written comments in MS.B tell us that he was producing ideal schemes for stables, for cities on rivers and canals, for temporary wooden architecture, and so on. The fact that all the comments are written backwards indicates that they were for private use only (note that Leonardo did not always use backwards writing: on some maps he wrote the right way round, obviously because he wanted to present them to other people). Furthermore, the fact that he drew 'in series' in MS.B, producing endless variations on circular, octagonal or other polygonal plans, suggests that he was interested not in planning real churches but rather in the application of ideal patterns to such structures. He appears to have had no particular project in mind: simply the question in general. This guess is supported by aspects of Leonardo's graphic technique in MS.B: in a large number of cases, he used just two devices to show us churches - the ground-plan and the bird's eye view (e.g. **118;** and compare **133**). The ground-plan is essential since it gives the relative breadths, lengths and details of the first order; but it provides little information about the upper orders and practically nothing about the upper exterior or interior and the roof levels. This is where the bird's eye view is so useful: Leonardo's aerial views show buildings tipped slightly forward, and tells us in general, but not in detail, practically all we need to know about the upper exteriors. Where Leonardo differs so drastically in drawing technique from his contemporaries lies in the fact that he practically never used their favourite, illustrative device - the interior perspective.

These drawings could indeed be imagined as preliminary sketches for a

94

model; but what is curious about them is that they are rarely accompanied by interior elevations, which are essential, and never by drawings of details or indications of dimensions. Moreover, none of them are labelled as projects, so that they look like a string of studies of exterior masses rather than anything else. The only conclusion possible is that the drawings in MS.B were not projects to be presented to a patron, thence to be visualised in a model and built by the labour force. The fact - frequently remarked upon - that at several points the buildings in MS.B look like real buildings does not necessarily mean that he was planning the Duomo at Pavia, the re-vamping of S. Satiro, or a Sforza Tomb (at all three of which he would, in any case, be almost entirely undocumented). Rather it indicates that, since all his plans were centralized or centralized and longitudinal, some of them were bound to look like some such building, or he found that he could incorporate some of the characteristics of real buildings in his ideal series.

Leonardo intended to produce treatises on various subjects, and Heydenreich long ago suggested that that was the function of MS.B. If so, the following may be observed: first, that MS.B as it stands is nowhere near ready since very few buildings have explanatory notes, the notes are written backwards and are of varying completeness, and the MS contains other types of material as well. Second, if Leonardo intended to work up the material to make it more like the Codex Madrid (which has many sheets with the text written out carefully into neat rectangles), and possibly as a presentation copy for a prospective patron, then the treatise would have been very different from those of Giuliano da Sangallo, Francesco di Giorgio and the author of the Codex Coner. Their works have very little text on the sheets with the drawings, and mainly present things that exist in enough detail to show architects everything they would need: that is, they were intended as copy-books, particularly illustrating ancient structures and all the essential details thereof. Leonardo's treatise would have included a great deal of text, of extreme practicality, presenting not things that exist but ideal projects for the way in which things ought to exist. That is, a treatise on architecture more like Serlio's in appearance with drawings embedded in the text. Quite clearly the majority of Leonardo's drawings, when they cannot be connected with specific projects, or identified as copies of things that exist, have this private, unresolved and meditative quality. Architecture was just one of Leonardo's many interests, and a minor one at that, especially later in his life. It tended to be a mirror, where it was like contemporary architecture, rather than a trend setter: sometimes up-to-date, but often stuck in the past.

Richard Schofield

# 'What men saw': Vasari's Life of Leonardo da Vinci and the image of the Renaissance artist

"To be or not to be, that is the question."
(William Shakespeare, *Hamlet*, III.i)

But what of coming to be? That is like Hamlet, his remark, or its author, becoming a form of cultural commonplace, recognisable, resonant, even in the most improbable context or unlikely presentation. Only by the crudest categorisation are Leonardo or his *Mona Lisa* a person and a portrait, for example. Their survival and their present identity is due to their transcendence of the particular of circumstance and their association with general, yet vital, cultural values. They have become symbols or metaphors. To study them is to engage with the systems of meaning that allow them to be understood in a certain moment and in a certain fashion. Put one way, why should we care about a long dead left-handed Italian vegetarian (any more than for the musings of an Englishman's version of a doubt-ridden Dane in a doublet)? The interest arises from the representative nature of these figures, taken to embody values that match and confirm basic themes that organise and characterise cultural understanding. To examine the origins and nature of the historical image of Leonardo in his earliest extended biography is to consider the conventions of being, that is of existing in a time and also being granted values that live beyond it - of being significant and becoming famous.

Renaissance biography was a commemorative art. Its aim was to preserve and to exalt the names and deeds of worthy men in order to provide examples, both of actions and of their rewards. This traditional, classical, notion of the form explains its attraction for Vasari. It served his purpose when he undertook to write about his profession in order to preserve the memory of his fellow artists and to glorify their art (Vasari 1, pp.9-10).[1] By organising information about the arts into a series of lives, following revered and recognisable biographical and rhetorical structures, he was automatically creating heroes. He adapted the mode of Plutarch (who wrote of rulers) to what had been the subject matter of Pliny (natural history). The essential truth of his history was not in its details, although he took pains to collect his information and to defend its accuracy; instead it was in its arrangement. The artifice is evident - intentionally so, for it transformed unstructured events into instructive examples (Vasari 3, pp.3-4). The facts of each Life were selected in order to demonstrate the ways and means of exercising virtue. They were

---

[1] All quotations from Vasari's *Lives* are the author's translations from the text as published in the 1966-87 edition by P. Barocchi and R. Bettarini (see bibliography, below p.109). For full references, see the version of this lecture published in *Art History* 13, 1990, pp.34-46.

subordinated to topics and themes that granted them value. What was important was not what had happened, but what could be considered worthy of mention.

One of the principal themes, indeed the motivating force of the *Lives* in general, is fame itself; and this key topic is featured in Leonardo's Life. Vasari wrote that:

"... the fame of his name became so great, that it was not only honoured in his time, but increased in posterity after his death." (Vasari 4, p.15)

In the first edition of the Life, Vasari elaborated on this:

"And truly the heavens occasionally send us some who represent not only humanity, but divinity itself, so that from this, as from a model, by imitating it, we can approach the highest parts of heaven with our mind and with the excellence of the intellect." (Vasari 4, pp.15-16)

Those who wished to follow in the footsteps of such "admirable spirits" through study, even if not aided by nature and unable to attain such greatness could "at least approach the divine works of those who partake of that divinity" (Vasari 4, p.16). It is ironic indeed that Leonardo, whose intellectual outlook was predominantly Aristotelian, should be presented or represented in the form of a neoplatonic ideal. Ironic, but not accidental. This obviously philosophical remark is a form of keynote, introducing a psychological/intellectual dimension to Vasari's portrayal of Leonardo, who is presented as a philosophising artist.

Vasari was quite deliberate in his choice of terms, and very consistent in his metaphorical constructions, even when mixing them as in this passage, where he has rendered concrete the supremely abstract goal offered by the neoplatonic model by which, through contemplation, the mind arrives at divinity. Spirit, soul and divinity are referred to a specific person, a set of works, a real model. Divinity can be approached, if not always achieved. Study replaces contemplation, and there is a path. There are traces, tracks, which can be followed. Greatness, supreme greatness, is put within sight.

The metaphor of path or way and attendant verbs (of following, moving) are important in the *Lives*. Vasari divided the history of the arts into three periods, beginning with the 'coarse', 'gross' age of Cimabue and preceding to the 'glorious', 'modern' one of Leonardo, Raphael, Michelangelo and eventually Vasari himself. Architecture, painting and sculpture are described as progressing from a dark, ignorant and imperfect time to one of consummate perfection. Artists and their accomplishments provided the 'lights'; so Cimabue "was born... to give the first lights to the art of painting", which guided the way (Vasari 2, p.35). And the artists of the third period were beneficiaries of the second, "they could, by means of that light rise and arrive at the height of perfection" (Vasari 4, p.3). The notion of way gives the assembled biographies a momentum. The imagery of light provides both a means and an end. For light and splendour, which make the artists literally luminaries, were recognisably words borrowed from a neoplatonic vocabulary. They were associated with the supreme intelligence, the source of light, the Creator. The metaphorical system used by Vasari was one that associated artists and their art with the most elevated forms of endeavour.

The rhetorical strategy that Vasari used to articulate this was based on hyperbole. According to the classical precepts that were the reference points for Vasari and his contemporaries, hyperbole was:

> "a virtue... when the magnitude of the facts passes all words, and in such circumstances our language will be more effective if it goes beyond the truth than if it falls short of it."[2]

The obvious exaggeration of Leonardo's gifts suggests their true magnitude. 'What men saw' in Leonardo in the celestial combination of beauty, grace and virtue well beyond the reach of human skill, was something literally inexpressible because it could not be reduced to the limitations of language (Vasari 4, p.15). In this way greatness itself was indicated, almost generically.

What does this serve? It was the function of hyperbole to inspire and direct imitation. The inherent idealism of the construction is based on what might be. No man can make himself be Leonardo or another Leonardo (that depends on fate), but by 'seeing' him as represented in this biography and by understanding the qualities of character listed and then exemplified in actions, there is the possibility of becoming like Leonardo. It was not worth his time, Vasari said, merely to state facts (Vasari 3, p.3). Recorded here is not only what happened, but what should have been and also what could come to pass. The strategic truths of this Life were intended to create possibilities for artists. The past serves as a form of backdrop to the stage of the future in a manner that parallels the function of the historical scenes which Vasari painted in the palaces of his patrons.

The rhetorical mode Vasari adopted in the *Lives* was that of the oratory of praise (epideictic or *genus demonstrativum*). The basic scheme of the individual Lives was derived from epideictic orations, that is, celebratory speeches. This branch of rhetoric concentrated on virtue, making deeds evidence for character and seeking to persuade or prompt the listener to admiration and to imitation. Immortality and example were both served by

---

[2] Quintilian, *Institutio oratoria* VIII, vi, 76; trans. H.M. Butler, Cambridge (Mass.) 1921, IV, pp.344-5.

this type of oratory, which gave great importance to form. Eloquence was its own impressive message. Vasari described Leonardo as initiating the modern style, and duly used terms and constructions expressive of the grace, order and powerful charm of that style. Given the key position of the Leonardo Life at the opening of the third age, it is not surprising that this should be a model biography for a model artist. As originally written it was rigorously structured with a eulogistic opening, an account of ancestry, birth and youth and choice of profession followed by works and deeds selected to illustrate the virtues of character, a moving death scene, a summary of accomplishments, celebratory epitaphs and a list of followers. Based on classical models, the form would have been readily discernible and appreciated by the contemporary reader, in itself conferring dignity on its subject by applying a pattern usually reserved for princes, saints and scholars. This structure is somewhat obscured in the second edition, which was revised according to historiographic principles favouring a more encyclopaedic form of history. Vasari was very careful in editing the Life, however; the eulogistic opening was only slightly shortened and most of the original writing of the Life remained untouched. Its basic themes were amplified, not altered.

The opening paragraphs set out the themes or topics of praise describing the artist's character and therefore determine the course of his life (and also its place in the course of Vasari's history). The subjects of praise in an epideictic oration were defined in classical oratorical treatises as external circumstances, physical attributes and qualities of character. So in Leonardo's Life Vasari begins by observing how:

"Very great gifts can be seen to rain down from celestial influences into human bodies, many times naturally, and occasionally supernaturally; superabundantly concentrating in one single body beauty, grace and virtue..." (Vasari 4, p.15)

This is a statement of the external circumstances (fortune) that provide advantages. The importance given to Leonardo's beauty is explained by the value this had in encomium. The topic of physical attributes was an essential part of praise. "Impressiveness and beauty" served to the subject's credit and were part of the demonstration of virtue. Eulogy also explains the fact that Vasari emphasises "the more than infinite grace in his every action... joined with dexterity, spirit and valour, always regal and noble", for strength and agility were other traditional features of the physical attributes (*rerum corporis*) (Vasari 4, p.15). That Vasari's Leonardo should resemble Castiglione's ideal courtier is not coincidental. He names precisely those qualities valued as courtly, gentlemanly - thereby suggesting a new rank and a new role for the artist of the modern age. Castiglione argued that grace was an essential quality of the courtier, for grace generates grace.[3] This formulation of character locates the artist in Vasari's ideal social arena, the charmed and concentrated circle of the powerful élite.

Passages developing the topics of praise follow the introduction, beginning with external circumstances. In the Leonardo Life, as in the other Lives, Vasari focused on the circumstances of the artist's education (rather than lineage, for example). Following classical formulae such as those set out in the handbook *Rhetorica ad Herennium*, he uses this topic to show how Leonardo was honourably trained, and how (using the rhetorical device of comparison) he surpassed his masters. A few months in the abacus school and he was confounding his teachers, a feat which, still a young lad, he was soon to repeat with Verrocchio, showing that in painting he knew more than his master (Vasari 4, pp.16 and 19). In addition to setting forth the conditions of Leonardo's education, Vasari enlarges upon his qualities of character and how they operated with respect to the external circumstances: his intellect "so divine and marvellous" that he was able to work in all the arts in which "design played a part" (Vasari 4, pp.16 and 17). He was "so pleasing in his conversation that he attracted men's souls to him", with the result that even without great income he had servants and horses. He could silence the learned and persuade the sober citizens of Florence that it was possible to raise the Baptistery into the air (Vasari 4, pp.18-19). Vasari concludes the opening, which advances and accumulates force through the repetition of Leonardo's perfections, with an assessment of his character and his career as was called for by panegyric. The final remarks have a somewhat negative aspect as:

> "One sees that Leonardo began many things with his knowledge of art and never finished any of them, as it seemed to him that the hand could not reach to the perfection of art in the things that he imagined." (Vasari 4, p.19)

This demonstrates the objectivity required of the historian, who must appraise as well as praise his subject. It also tempers Leonardo's heavenliness, so different in kind from Michelangelo's unalloyed divinity, an important, implicit comparison in the structure of the *Lives*, which were meant to culminate in the figure of Michelangelo. And it also seems to have been the case.

Leonardo was not only a subject of Vasari's history. He was subjected to history. Vasari never intended to produce an inventory. He found (or invented, to use the appropriate rhetorical term) the major themes that were embodied

---

[3] For this quality and its effect, see E. Saccone, "*Grazia, Sprezzatura, Affettazione* in the *Courtier*", in *Castiglione: The Ideal and the Real in Renaissance Culture*, ed. R.W. Hanning and D. Rosand, New Haven and London 1983, pp.45-67.

and exemplified in the lives and the persons of the artists he described. Events were made to confirm laws of behaviour, general principles of action and consequences, rules and standards. Verbs of demonstration (*mostrare, dimostrare, fece vedere, fece conoscere*) are used throughout to create constructions of proof essential to this formulaic structuring. Vasari's success as an artist and author was based on working the system; that is mastering the conventions of social exchange and using them to his advantage. Vasari's stock of ideas about things like education (choice of good master, the rewards of diligence and study), talent (given by nature, need for nurture), the importance of competition (as opposed to the deplorable effects of envy), the desire to demonstrate *virtù* and gain honour, the mutual respect (love) of artist and patron, were drawn from the thematic repertory of the period. He not only employed them in biography but in his own life: in the letters he wrote, in his own studies and his production of paintings. Derived in great part from classical literature and art, they had the status of canon, or paradigm, providing both form and authority that were acceptable and desirable.

These conventions were the currency of the society Vasari wished to serve, the quite select and quite specific élite associated with the ducal and papal courts of his time. These men were the wealthy, educated and influential who operated with increasingly conscious and functional notions of self (as courtier, cardinal, or prince, for example) and who maintained control on the means of representation: the printing presses as well as the building and decoration of palaces, the embellishment of churches and all forms of public and private ceremony. Vasari's *Lives*, for example, were printed first by the Torrentino (1550) and then by the Giunti (1568) presses; both operated under licence to Duke Cosimo de'Medici. The *Lives* were a form of public relations exercise addressed to this circle of interested parties. They were meant to be convincing, to engage attention, to confirm and establish connections: one of which was to make definitive the association of the artist with high culture, his work an embodiment of the principal ideals of the period. This was effectively the creation of the renaissance artist. The desire to persuade is also a measure of accuracy. The truth of the *Lives* relates as much to the intended result as to the underlying matter of fact.

In the case of Leonardo, what were the facts? When Vasari wrote the first edition of the Life in the mid 1540s in Rome and Florence, the stock was limited indeed. Vasari knew Leonardo more through his reputation than through any of his works; but that was quite considerable. One source was Paolo Giovio, Vasari's friend and supporter, who, like Leonardo, had been at the court of Pope Leo X. Giovio had written brief eulogistic accounts of Leonardo, Michelangelo and Raphael (all had been at the papal court). These were important as both inspiration and source for Vasari who was aided in writing the *Lives* by Giovio. In fact, in his autobiography he claimed that the original idea for the book was Giovio's (Vasari 6, pp.389-90). It is in Giovio's eulogy that the extraordinarily handsome, affable, generous, lute-playing, philosophising artist makes a first appearance. He was also presented as the intelligent, curious artist who:

> "giving himself over with excessive meticulousness to searching for new technical means for a refined art, finished very few works, always discarding ideas due to inconstancy of character and innate impatience."[4]

These qualities of character, the topics of Giovio's eulogy, became the basis of Vasari's portrait of the artist. He was careless of such details as Giovio's brief biography supplied him and more complimentary to the artist, a not untypical relation of Vasari to a learned adviser.

Giovio had also treated of Leonardo, Michelangelo and Raphael in what was planned to be a treatise on literary style. Never completed, one of the surviving fragments uses this triad in a discussion of imitation and creative procedure. Giovio placed them against Perugino:

> "Who has ever practiced painting... with more success and fame than Perugino... But after those bright lights of a perfect art called Vinci, Michelangelo and Raphael suddenly emerged from the shadow of that age, they eclipsed his fame... with their marvellous works."[5]

Vasari was also to oppose Perugino and those luminaries. In the first edition of the Lives, Perugino was the last artist treated in the second age, as one unable to understand the new art. This rather downbeat ending to the epoch was modified in the second edition, where Vasari used his mentor Signorelli to presage the coming glory. In chronological and in contemporary terms the division between Leonardo and Perugino is a false one. They were of the same generation, both had been apprenticed to Verrocchio and were paired in appreciation by their patrons and fellow painters. It was Giovio who first put Perugino into the shadow of a new type of artist or artistry, a separation Vasari was to accept and develop when he ordered the artists "according to the order of styles rather than time" and placed Leonardo as the first of the moderns (Vasari 2, p.32).

For other information about Leonardo, Vasari could refer to the attribution of the angel in Verrocchio's *Baptism of Christ* (**fig.20**) to Leonardo, recorded

---

[4] Translated from P.Barocchi (ed.), *Scritti d'arte del Cinquecento*, Turin 1977, I, p.8.

[5] Translated from Barocchi 1977, I, p.19.

in an early 16th century guidebook to Florence.[6] He knew works owned by Florentine collectors, like his honoured friend Ottaviano de'Medici who had a cartoon for a tapestry showing the *Expulsion from Paradise* (Vasari gave his friend pride of place by making this the second work mentioned in the Life, just after the angel in the *Baptism*), or the drawing of *Neptune* that had passed from the Segni family to Giovanni Gaddi, and was celebrated by an epigram by the academician Fabio Segni, which Vasari quoted. Vasari's sources were relatively limited and his biases were resolutely Florentine. It is worth noting that there are many ways in which we know Leonardo and Vasari did not, or did not choose to. He commissioned epitaphs from academicians, we read contracts and letters and commemorative verses from the Sforza court. Vasari did not cite the passages in the treatise *De Scultura* (1504) by Pomponius Gauricus, or Luca Pacioli's 1509 treatise *De Divina Proportione*, which were available to him as well as to us. But he did know Leonardo in ways that we cannot. Friends and acquaintances of Vasari's - Gianfrancesco Rustici, Pontormo, Baccio Bandinelli - had known Leonardo and could supply their reminiscences. And there were certainly echoes of Leonardo's words still to be caught in Florence in the 1520s when Vasari arrived there. For many of Vasari's generalisations in the *Lives* about art, nature, poetry, imitation are similar to those found in Leonardo's notebooks. These originate in a shared tradition of thought about the arts, one that Vasari could appropriately refer to Leonardo, who was a contributor. And this extremely elusive trace of an influential presence is important to remember - it was the living source of the reputation that formed the basis of Leonardo's fame and the reconstruction of the person in Vasari's biography.

This Life was greatly expanded in its second edition. Following the editorial criteria proposed to Vasari by Vincenzo Borghini, Vasari sought out new information to made additions and corrections. He visited Milan briefly but purposefully in May 1566, one stop on what was a form of research tour for the second edition. There he visited Leonardo's student, Francesco Melzi, who cherished Leonardo's notebooks like relics. He learned about the plan for a book on anatomy. In Florence he was approached by a Milanese artist (whose name he seems to have forgotten, leaving a tantalising blank in the text), who wanted to print Leonardo's writings on painting (Vasari 4, p.28). He had become a collector of drawings and was a promoter and founding member of the Florentine Accademia del Disegno, interests manifest in his account of the notebooks and of Leonardo's drawing procedures and activities as a draughtsman. He writes of the drapery studies on linen (he had one in his *libro de' disegni*), and of bizarre heads that he had copied, and also of

---

[6]   F. Albertini, "Memoriale di Molte Statue et Picture sono nella inclyta Cipta di Florentia...", Rome 1510; see *Five Early Guides to Rome and Florence*, ed. P. Murray, Westmead, Farnborough, Hants., 1972 (unpaginated).

architectural and engineering schemes and machines of all sorts: "of such thoughts and labours one sees many drawings scattered throughout our profession, and I have seen a considerable number of them" (Vasari 4, p.18). Typically he added works in the collection of his employer, Duke Cosimo de'Medici (a pointing angel and a *Medusa*); and in other private collections, including the unfinished *Adoration of the Magi* (**fig.16**) that was in the house of Amerigo Benci (Vasari 4, pp.23 and 24). He is somewhat more precise about historical circumstances (Vasari 4, p.24). *Le Novelle* by Matteo Bandello (published in 1554) had come to his attention. These stories included the anecdote about Leonardo and the prior of Sta Maria delle Grazie that Vasari paraphrased, using it as an opportunity for the artist to speak a pleasing discourse to the Duke on the subject of the inventive, intellectual nature of art (Vasari 4, pp.25-6). These additions enhance, they do not change Vasari's original portrayal. In revising this Life, Vasari seems to have taken great care to do so in a way that reinforced the previously established themes. The Life retains its exemplary status as a piece of historical writing, correct in the current mode.

Vasari's Leonardo is a fabrication, not a fiction. In his dedicatory letter to Duke Cosimo, Vasari stated that he undertook the task of presenting the example of such worthy men with the accuracy and fidelity required by the truth of history (Vasari 1, p.3). What was true must also be lifelike. The means of bringing a legend to life were suggested by Plutarch in the introduction to his biographies of Alexander the Great and Julius Caesar:

> "the most brilliant exploits often tell us nothing of the virtues or vices of the men who performed them, while on the other hand a chance remark or a joke may reveal far more of a man's character... When a portrait painter sets out to create a likeness, he relies above all upon the face and the expression of the eyes and pays less attention to the other parts of the body; in the same way it is my task to dwell upon those actions which illuminate the workings of the soul, and by this means to create a portrait of each man's life."[7]

Portraits were valued precisely because they made the absent present. And Vasari (3, p.201), like Leonardo,[8] felt that every artist portrayed himself. His notion of life style was a comprehensive style of being, all acts (and works) were representative: an artist was what he created. One of the qualities that

---

[7] Plutarch, *The Age of Alexander*, trans. I. Scott-Kilvert, Harmondsworth 1973, p.252.

[8] See M. Kemp, "*Ogni dipintore dipinge sè*. A Neoplatonic Echo in Leonardo's Art Theory?", *Cultural Aspects of the Italian Renaissance. Essays in Honour of Paul Oscar Kristeller*, ed. C. Clough, Manchester 1976, pp.311-23.

Vasari most admired in Leonardo was his diligence in depiction, his ability to "counterfeit all of the details of nature exactly as they are" and to give "his figures motion and breath" (Vasari 4, p.18). In this Life, Vasari is equally diligent in his attention to detail. The amount of incident is striking and Leonardo's works are described in terms of their stories, emphasizing their expressiveness. The power of words was Leonardo's: Vasari says that he was pleasing in conversation, convincing in argument (Vasari 4, p.17). Vasari's information may have been in some measure anecdotal, which would have influenced his presentation of Leonardo, but this portrayal is also based on an awareness of the naturalistic power of storytelling.

The order in portraying a life according to Vasari's rhetorical models was to pass from the topics of praise to the narrative of deeds, and this was the order he observed. The first of the illustrative deeds is recounted as the tale of the peasant and the painted shield. Vasari introduces this as a story: *Dicesi*, 'it is said'. It takes the form of a *beffa*, a practical joke, a favoured type of storytelling in Florence. In fact there is triple duplicity. One of ser Piero's farmers had cut a roundel from a fig tree and wanted to have it painted in Florence. Ser Piero was willing to oblige a faithful servant and took it to Leonardo, who smoothed and shaped the rough panel and then filled his room with:

> "lizards, crickets, serpents, butterflies, locusts, bats and other strange kinds of similar animals, from this multitude, variously combined, he created a horrible and fearsome monster which poisoned the air with its breath and turned the air to flames..."
> (Vasari 4, p.21)

So great was the love he bore art, Vasari says, that he did not notice the stench of the dead animals. When ser Piero came to collect the finished work, Leonardo arranged it on a stand, bathed in light. His unsuspecting father was so startled that he ran way thinking the monster to be real. Leonardo held him back, telling him to take it away for it had fulfilled its purpose (Vasari 4, p.22). It seemed a miracle to ser Piero who praised his son's capricious speech and bought his farmer a ready-made and quite commonplace roundel from a small goods merchant. He secretly sold Leonardo's for one hundred ducats to merchants who in turn received three hundred from the Duke of Milan. The joke is first on Leonardo's father, then on the peasant and finally on Leonardo. Each was taken in: the father by the reality of the painting, the peasant by the painting received and Leonardo by the sale and resale of the shield. But each was also pleased by the result and shown in their true character: a certain simplicity with respect to understanding art (and art commerce apparently) on the part of father and farmer, a total indifference to market value on the part of Leonardo. The story serves to demonstrate Leonardo's absorption in his art and his notion of its purpose. The true deception was not that played by ser Piero on the peasant or his son, but Leonardo's with respect to reality. Yet even as he praises this remarkable devotion to art, Vasari calls it into question. The joke form of the tale subtly undermines Leonardo, conveying the message that art has more serious purposes - and that such love should be turned to producing works for suitable clients, for important sites and of subjects truly worthy of record.

In the subsequent narration of works, Vasari shows Leonardo to be quite capable of meeting such challenges and being duly rewarded by fame. His descriptions, some quite circumstantial, are often representative reconstructions. Vasari had probably seen very few of Leonardo's works (as most were not done, destroyed or distant); but because what is being given is as much an evaluation or evocation as illustrative description, it was possible for Vasari to give accounts of works he knew by reputation rather than by sight or study. In this connection it should be remembered that his book was illustrated by portraits of the artists, not their works. Throughout the *Lives* Vasari was relying upon the imaginative faculty of memory. The *Mona Lisa* (**fig.4**) for example, was in France. Known to him through copy drawings or copies, Vasari brings the painting to the reader's mind in vivid detail. He praises it as something seen as exemplary:

> "Who wished to see how closely art could imitate nature, could easily understand it in this head, because there were counterfeited all the details that could be painted with subtle skill..." (Vasari 4, p.30)

What follows is a catalogue of the subtleties of the rendering of the features, her brow, her eyes, nose, neck - the skin not painted, but flesh itself. Vasari reproduces the pulse of the painting. It is a lover's lyric. The parallels are clearly Petrarchan, calling to mind the most famous painting in the poetry of the Renaissance, Simone Martini's portrait of Laura. And it is likely that Vasari was consciously echoing that tradition, describing the *Mona Lisa* in terms taken from the literature of love and its poetic ideals of beauty (see Kemp 1981, pp.267-8).

Given the fact that the artist was described as divine in every action it is logical that his works were seen to be marvels and marvellous. These terms occur repeatedly, applied for example to the *Last Supper* (**fig.25**) and the (now lost) *Virgin and Child with St Anne* cartoon. In both cases the public reacted with veneration. For two days the Florentines, men and women, old and young, went to see the cartoon "as one goes to solemn feasts", instead witnessing the marvels of Leonardo (Vasari 4, p.29). Another key theme is that of nobility. This was important to Vasari who was seeking to counter a stereotype of the artist as bizarre and uncouth with a new well-mannered model of artist for the modern age, hence this emphasis in the first biography of the third era. Leonardo's association with the highest levels of society is constantly noted as he matches and meets rank with talent. The nobility of the *Last Supper* made the French king desire to take it back to his kingdom without regard for the expense (Vasari 4, p.26). The works Vasari mentions in the Life are usually associated with noteworthy owners: prestigious provenances are the norm.

This topic of nobility has its culmination in the scene of Leonardo's death in the arms of the King of France. In his last moments the artist showed contrition:

> "for how greatly he had offended God and the men of this world, not having worked in his art as was proper. Whence came a paroxysm, messenger of death; whereupon the king rose and took his head to help him and ease his distress; his spirit, which was most divine, knowing that there could be no greater honour, expired..." (Vasari 4, p.36)

The moving and totally apocryphal scene is a happy resolution of the difficulty of Leonardo's life. Leonardo seems to have lived the contradiction of the psychology of his time. What was truly creative, imaginative, could never, by definition be realised. To make a mental image material was to debase it. This was a critical issue for Vasari as well. His argument, which was also Leonardo's, was that overcoming the limitations of the material in order to make such images manifest was a demonstration of the creative genius of the artist. When Vasari measured Leonardo according to his talents, there was no boundary, but when he applied the judgment of a practising painter, there was the regretful conclusion that Leonardo had betrayed that talent. By making Leonardo repent on his deathbed Vasari forced a recognition of this. The final scene becomes a form of apotheosis. It brings together nobility of birth and the transcending nobility of spirit. This is true historical portrayal, depicting an episode impossible in fact, but probable in circumstance and logical given the topics of praise informing the biography.

Vasari's Leonardo, although divine, was not perfect. That Vasari was not troubled by this seeming contradiction is due to his understanding of the spirit of history which taught "men to live and made them prudent" (Vasari 3, p.4). His intention was to create an instrument of judgment by giving models for appraisal and action. The reading of the *Lives* was not conceived of as passive. The relation of past to present was interactive: one was meant to influence the other. Vasari did not expect the heavens to favour the earth with a constant downpour of the extraordinary gifts that were embodied in Leonardo (however much he would have welcomed such a phenomenon). Instead he suggests that such cases should be recognised mimetically, as forming an image of the artist reflected in the mirror of history. The virtues of such a figure, once recorded (made representative) became imitable. And the faults could be corrected. In Leonardo's case the faults were exactly those amenable to human skills (*arte umana*) - that is, getting on with the work. Furthermore in tempering Leonardo's divinity with humanity, Vasari granted him life as well as fame. He became vivid through the details of description, a form of attraction Vasari knew well from the literary and pictorial traditions he combined as artist and author.[9]

With Vasari's biography Leonardo entered history as a charming, complex and compelling character. He was associated with the highest goals of art and with the marvellous powers needed to investigate them. The artist as represented by Vasari in Leonardo was removed from the constraints of traditional social and professional categories. He was to be evaluated in terms of the expression of his genius and the aspirations of his work. Underlying this presentation is the notion that these things were desirable, useful and honourable. And so it seems they were. The element of recognition on which Vasari based this biography, on 'what men saw', is one of cultural complicity, which granted this Life a plausibility and persuasiveness as enduring and attractive as its subject.

Patricia Rubin

---

[9] See S.L. Alpers, "*Ekphrasis* and aesthetic attitudes in Vasari's *Lives*", *Journal of the Warburg and Courtauld Institutes* XXIII, 1960, pp.190-212.

# Bibliography

Calder 1970

R. Calder, *Leonardo and the Age of the Eye*, London 1970

Catalogue 1989

M. Kemp and J. Roberts, *Leonardo da Vinci: Artist - Scientist - Inventor* (exhibition catalogue), London 1989

Clark 1976

K. Clark, *Leonardo da Vinci*, Harmondsworth 1976

Clark/Pedretti 1968

K. Clark and C. Pedretti, *The Drawings of Leonardo da Vinci in the Collection of Her Majesty the Queen at Windsor Castle*, 2nd ed., London 1968 (2 vols)

Clark/Pedretti 1969

K. Clark and C. Pedretti, *The Drawings of Leonardo da Vinci in the Collection of Her Majesty the Queen at Windsor Castle*, vol.3: Anatomical Manuscripts A,B and C, 2nd ed., London 1969

Goldscheider 1943

L. Goldscheider, *Leonardo da Vinci*, London 1943

Janson 1963

H. W. Janson, *The Sculpture of Donatello*, Princeton 1963

Keele 1983

K. D. Keele, *Leonardo da Vinci's Elements of the Science of Man*, London 1983

Kemp 1981

M. Kemp, *Leonardo da Vinci: the marvellous works of Man and Nature*, London 1981

Kemp/Walker 1989

M. Kemp and M. Walker, *Leonardo On Painting*, New Haven and London 1989

McMahon 1956

Leonardo da Vinci, *Treatise on Painting*, ed. A. P. McMahon, Princeton 1956

Passavant 1969

G. Passavant, *Verrocchio*, London 1969

Pedretti 1986

C. Pedretti, *Leonardo Architect*, London 1986

Pope-Hennessy 1963

J. Pope-Hennessy, *Italian High Renaissance and Baroque Sculpture*, 3 vols., London 1963

Pope-Hennessy 1971

J. Pope-Hennessy, *Italian Renaissance Sculpture*, 2nd ed., London 1971

Popham 1946

A. E. Popham, *The Drawings of Leonardo da Vinci*, London 1946

Reti ed. 1974

ed. L. Reti, *The Unknown Leonardo*, London 1974

Richter 1970

J. P. Richter, *The Literary works of Leonardo da Vinci*, 2nd ed., London 1970 (2 vols)

Royal Academy 1977

*Leonardo da Vinci: Anatomical Drawings from the Royal Collection (exhibition catalogue)*, London (Royal Academy of Arts) 1977

Vasari

G. Vasari, *Le Vite...*, eds. P. Barocchi and R.Bettarini, Florence 1966-87

Vasari/Bull 1971

G. Vasari, *Lives of the Artists*, trans. G. Bull, Harmondsworth 1971

## Abbreviated references to Leonardo's manuscripts and drawings

| | |
|---|---|
| BL | London, British Library (Codex Arundel) |
| BN 2038 | Paris, Institut de France (MS Ashburnham II) |
| CA | Milan, Biblioteca Ambrosiana, Codex Atlanticus |
| Forster I, II and III | London, Victoria and Albert Museum, Library, Codex Forster I-III |
| Hammer (formerly Codex Leicester) | Los Angeles, Armand Hammer Collection, Codex Hammer |
| Madrid I and II | Biblioteca Nacional, MSS 8937 and 8936 |
| MSS A to M | Paris, Institut de France, Leonardo Manuscripts A to M |
| Urb | Vatican, Codex Urbinas Latinus 1270 |
| Windsor | Royal Library, Collection of Her Majesty The Queen |

For full bibliographical references to publications of these manuscripts, see Kemp/Walker 1989, pp.317-8.

# Index of names

# Index of Leonardo's major works